PRA

"Michelle Arb   n-
bers with intui̶ŧ̶ï̶v̶e̶ ̶g̶e̶n̶i̶u̶s̶.̶ ̶S̶h̶e̶ i̶s̶ a natural guiding teacher."
                              —Carrie White, celebrity stylist and author of
                                    Upper Cut: Highlights of My Hollywood Life

"Michelle has a rare gift as a communicator and I am always
impressed by her amazing spiritual insight. This book is a great
read."
                         —Treva Etienne, film and television actor with roles in
                                     Pirates of the Caribbean and *Criminal Minds*

"Quite simply, Michelle Arbeau delivers like no one else can."
                              —Ricky Powell, founder of lifelonghappiness.com

"This is a book we can all learn from as it guides us to knowing
our inner thoughts and outer reactions. I am impressed."
                         —Sharon Quirt, co-author of *The Keys: Open the Door
                                to True Empowerment and Infinite Possibilities*

the
Energy
of
Words

About the Author

Michelle Arbeau is an internationally recognized celebrity numerologist, author, inspirational speaker, and radio/tv host. She has a client base that includes various famous actors and actresses, Hollywood directors, celebrity stylists, and many more. A media favorite and considered an expert in her field, Michelle is frequently a guest on CBC Radio and on programs such as CTV *Morning Live* and *Breakfast Television*.

As founder and host of Authentic You Radio/TV, Michelle has interviewed many top authors, speakers, and celebrities in her quest to inspire and empower others to live with authenticity.

Use the Vibration of Language
to Manifest the Life You Desire

the Energy of Words

MICHELLE ARBEAU

Llewellyn Publications
Woodbury, Minnesota

First Edition
Sixth Printing, 2019

Background image: iStockphoto.com/139915/Dominic Current
Cover design by Ellen Lawson

Library of Congress Cataloging-in-Publication Data
Arbeau, Michelle, 1978–
   The energy of words : use the vibration of language to manifest the
life you desire / Michelle Arbeau. — First Edition.
      page   cm.
   Includes bibliographical references.
   ISBN 978-0-7387-3664-8
1. Lexicology—Psychological aspects. 2. Phraseology. 3.
Psycholinguistics. I. Title.
   P326.5.P75A73 2013
   420.1'9—dc23
                              2013029882

Llewellyn Worldwide Ltd. does not participate in, endorse, or have any authority or responsibility concerning private business transactions between our authors and the public.
   All mail addressed to the author is forwarded, but the publisher cannot, unless specifically instructed by the author, give out an address or phone number.
   Any Internet references contained in this work are current at publication time, but the publisher cannot guarantee that a specific location will continue to be maintained. Please refer to the publisher's website for links to authors' websites and other sources.

Llewellyn Publications
A Division of Llewellyn Worldwide Ltd.
2143 Wooddale Drive
Woodbury, MN 55125-2989
www.llewellyn.com

Printed in the United States of America

OTHER BOOKS BY MICHELLE ARBEAU

Soul Numbers: Decipher the Messages from
Your Inner Self to Successfully Navigate Life
(Premier Digital Publishing)

Special thanks to my friend and earth angel Michelle Russell for helping me plant the seed for the vision of my life's work.

CONTENTS

Foreword

"CHANGE YOUR WORDS, CHANGE YOUR REALITY"
—Marie D. Jones

"In the beginning was the word..."

One does not have to follow a particular religious tradition to see the power of the spoken word in major belief systems. Spiritual masters have always known that words have the ability to create...and destroy. Some of the most beloved quotes, sayings, and proverbs speak of this creative power, urging us to choose our words wisely and align our words to our actions; the law of the universe is one of vibration, resonance, and attraction.

What we say is what we see.

What we tell ourselves over and over again becomes our reality.

Ancient and indigenous cultures alike understood that what you named a thing was as critical as the thing itself. Aboriginal cultures sang things into existence by naming them. At birth we are given a special "identity" through our names. Like numbers, the chosen language of the universe, words have a secret and hidden power to shape and mold physical reality itself. How little do we understand this power and how rarely do we use it to our advantage.

I have written a number of books that explore the power of numbers, words, and symbols and how they influence our perception of the world around us. In *The Resonance Key: Exploring the Links Between Vibration, Consciousness, and the Zero Point Grid* (New Page Books, 2009), my coauthor Larry Flaxman and I examine how sound has been a creative force throughout history, associated with everything from the building of great edifices like the pyramids to healing the body of illness with various resonances and frequencies. In *The Trinity Secret: The Power of Three and the Code of Creation* (New Page Books, 2011), I explore how the law of attraction works and why what we speak becomes what we attract, good or bad. In *The Déjà Vu Enigma: A Journey Through the Anomalies of Mind, Memory, and Time* (New Page Books, 2010), I discuss at length the power of the word, both written and spoken, to create, heal, and even kill. You can pray someone into healing or you can curse someone into illness and even death … if you truly believe in the power of words.

What we say to others, and even more importantly what we say to ourselves, has a resonance, a vibrational frequency that is put out into the world. This frequency lingers and has a far greater effect than we imagine. Words of love inspire and empower. Words of hate destroy and diminish. Experiments with water crystals and plants have shown that what we say literally changes the physical and molecular form of that at which we direct our words. Words have won wars, caused great chaos, lifted nations up from devastation, urged on champions, and both united and divided populaces.

Once we establish that words are far more than just a form of communication, we need to look at how they can be used to make our lives better. For what good is knowledge if it cannot be applied to our own individual day-to-day lives for the purpose of growth, enlightenment, and improvement? In *The Energy of Words: Use the Vibration of Language to Manifest the Life You Desire*, author and celebrity numerologist Michelle Arbeau has created a powerful guide to examining how we use and even abuse words, as well as how we can teach ourselves to make better choices when it comes to how we talk to ourselves, others, and even the world around us. Everything we think and speak is a cause with an effect. In order to improve the effects in our lives, we must improve the causes, and although we may not have control over everything we encounter in life, we do have control over the words we choose and the thoughts we think.

Michelle's understanding of the profound nature of numbers, words, and symbols makes her the perfect teacher to present these amazing lessons in shaping your reality through shifting your vibrational frequencies, and it's all so simple. If you change your words and thoughts, you change your reality. Yet the action steps often intimidate people into never making those changes, which is why a book like this is so inspiring and empowering. Someone has done the hard work for us and can now share the knowledge, techniques, and lessons that will get us from where we are to where we want to be.

Language is at the root of humanity's understanding and expression of itself. Our history as a species is a story we all tell ourselves, collectively adding to it as time progresses. Likewise, each person's individual history is an ongoing story. By looking into the root of language we can see into the past and peer into the future, yet none of that matters if we cannot find a way to make language and the words we speak work for us in the present. None of that matters if the stories we tell ourselves hold us back from a full expression of who we are and why we are here.

It all comes down to this: If you want to manifest more happiness, joy, prosperity, health, and blessings, you must change the way you think, speak, write, and express. If you want to express your fullest self and find your purpose and your destiny, you must change your vibration. If you want to truly live an authentic life, you must change your beliefs.

You must change your *words*.

Changing your words will transform you and, in turn, your reality.

Marie D. Jones (www.mariedjones.com), bestselling author of *Destiny Vs. Choice: The Scientific and Spiritual Evidence Behind Fate and Free Will* (New Page Books, 2011) and *The Resonance Key: Exploring the Links Between Vibration, Consciousness, and the Zero Point Grid* (New Page Books, 2009).

Introduction

You might have already read books on the law of attraction and feel like you have the steps down to a science. Do you find it never seems to work the way it should? Why do you think that is? The basics of this law are simple: what you send out to the universe, via your thoughts and intentions, you get back. Sounds like a piece of cake, but it's easier said than done. Most experts say your biggest hang-up is in doubting the process. However, the source of that doubt may be from an unsuspecting source—your words.

You speak, write, and think in words, but it's important to choose the right words. Negative words or words that don't resonate with your vibration are like energetic junk food. Creating the life you desire is more than just sending your wish list off to the universe. You can't manifest a life of joy and abundance if you're sending out the vibration of lacking and doubt through the words you choose. To be effective, *every* word you use needs to make you feel good.

The Energy of Words: Use the Vibration of Language to Manifest the Life You Desire is a guidebook for creating the life you've been dreaming of. This guide takes you through the process of using the creative power of words to transform your life. You will learn to uncover and eliminate negative vocabulary on all levels and replace it with positive, personalized lingo that will help you to thrive.

This book examines each word from three perspectives. The first perspective is the word's dictionary definition—what does the word mean to you and from a societal point of view? The second perspective is through numerology and numbers highlighting the frequency or vibration of a word from an energetic standpoint: Is it a positive or negative word? What is it energetically adding to or subtracting from the life you desire? The third perspective is based on the science of the law of attraction: Is the word's vibration in alignment with what you envision for your life? How can you shift your frequency through the words you choose to use in order to start attracting something different and more desirable?

Several books have touched on the vibrations of words, but interestingly, very few have delved deep into words' energies. The controversial book *Messages from Water* by Dr. Masaru Emoto (Hado Publishing, 1999) was the first of its kind to delve into the topic of the energetic power of language. Emoto's book is based on his scientific research demonstrating the effects of positive and negative words on water. When a word was spoken, written, or thought and directed at the water, the water responded by forming varying sizes and shapes of crystal clusters. His research and book have become very widely known, stirring up both curiosity and criticism around the world. *Messages from Water* offers evidence of the power of words from an energetic standpoint but stops short of showing us how we can practically apply these incredible findings to our own lives. This book you now have in your hands continues where Dr. Emoto left off, providing both further evidence of the vibration of words and how to effectively harness their powerful energy in practical and doable ways.

Before you delve into the book, I wish to clarify what numerology and the law of attraction are, as they are the underlying bases of the book. Numerology is the science of numbers from an energetic standpoint (not in the mathematical sense). The metaphysical community has believed for millennia that the world and everything in it is energy, and in recent decades the scientific community has made strides to prove this theory. Quantum physics has discovered that the base of an atom is not matter, but frozen light particles of energy. As the late Noble Peace Prize-winning physicist David Bohm wrote in his book *Wholeness and the Implicate Order*,[1] the universe is a sea of energy. Bohm saw the fundamental activity of nature as light; matter is not solid, but rather condensed light. In other words, atoms—the basis of all matter—are comprised of frozen or slowed light particles (energy).

Pythagoras, a Greek mathematician and philosopher in the late 500s BCE, became known as "the Father of Numbers." He discovered through his study of numbers that all things had a basis in number. Much of the knowledge of Pythagoras and information about his life was documented centuries after his death, so the accuracy of his work and theories has been questioned. One of the main pieces we know about Pythagoras is that he had a Mystery School where he taught that nothing could exist without numbers. He believed that mathematics formed the basis of all things in existence and that numbers were the essence of creation.

Based on the findings of Pythagoras, every number in existence is created from the base numbers 1–9, which are the numerical figures that form the basis of numerology. Drawing upon the theory that all things are energy at their core, numbers are also energy and can represent the energy patterns within and around us.

What is energy exactly? The mainstream scientific definition is that energy is "the ability to do work." There are two kinds of energy: "kinetic energy (energy of motion) or potential energy (stored energy of position)"[2]; an example of kinetic energy would be wind or running water while an example of potential energy would be static electricity.

In quantum physics, string theory takes the definition of energy a step further: "All objects in our universe are composed of vibrating filaments (strings) and membranes (branes) of energy."[3] This description of energy explains that all things are energy at their base, which is precisely why there is such power in all things. Even numbers and words have an energetic basis with the "ability to do work," as the widely accepted scientific definition of energy says. For this reason, words and numbers have an energetic effect on us.

In recent years, there has been overwhelming demand for information on numbers because many across the globe are seeing repeating number sequences, such as 11:11. This phenomenon has yet to be fully explained, but there are many theories in the metaphysical community presenting the idea that numerical patterns, like 11:11, are the codes of creation being revealed to those paying attention. These theories indicate that numbers are the language of the universe, and these numbers have the ability to reveal to us who we are, what we're here to do, and how to do it. Think of numbers as spiritual DNA. Anything in the world can be reduced to a base number or energetic frequency of 1–9. This base number code can tell you the spiritual or energetic essence of a person, place, or thing. This includes words, of course, which is the method through which this book is able to reveal the powerful energies of the words you choose to use and the impact they have on your own essence and the world around you.

This book is the culmination of my work with numbers and numerology and also my passion for words as an avid writer since I was a child. I want to share with you my personal journey with numbers and words and the connection between the two. I had the privilege of experiencing something early in life that I now consider a gift. It allowed me a brief window into the soulful world of spirit that not everyone has the opportunity to glimpse. At the age of four, I went through a near death experience (NDE) that sparked my curiosity for the unseen spirit world.

My mother was visiting her friend and I was playing with her sons down the hall. The boys and I were sharing a box of Gobstoppers candy when I suddenly began to choke on one. They thought I was joking and wouldn't let me out of the room for what seemed like an eternity. The room started to appear as though I was viewing it through a distorted bubble. By the time they let me out, I was barely clinging to life. The last thing I remember before passing out was making it into the hallway where my mother caught me in her arms.

My lips were blue, I wasn't breathing, and I was lying limp in my mother's arms. I remember vividly the experience of watching my mother, from outside my body, frantically attempting to remove the candy from my throat. The whole experience lasted for maybe three minutes, but the most prominent thing that stands out from that day was the incredible sense of calm and peace surrounding me after I left my body. As I watched the scene like a bystander, I felt no fear, anxiety, or sadness, just a profound sense of tranquility I'll never forget as long as I live.

There's another piece to this story that further solidifies my belief that there is more to life than what we can see with our human eyes. Standing on either side of me during that experience, while I was outside my body, were two beings made of white light. To this day, I still can't say for sure who or what they were, but I do know that they had no definitive shape and were the most brilliant white light I have ever seen. As bright as it was, it was not hard on my eyes or overpowering in any way. The enormous amount of serene energy and love emanating from them was a feeling unsurpassed in the human world. No love on earth can compare to the love I felt these beings had for me. I felt safe, loved, and totally at peace.

After that experience, I noticed I was more aware of the subtle aspects of life. I knew about people, places, or things that

I had no reasonable cause for knowing. I had seemingly random premonitions or visions. This continued throughout my childhood and into my early twenties until the next profound experience came that would officially mark my alignment with my life purpose.

About ten years ago, at the age of twenty-four, I suddenly began to dream in numbers every single night. I had always been a vivid dreamer because of my heightened connection to the spiritual realm, but this was something I had never experienced before. Over the course of several weeks, I filled a notepad with number messages that showed up in my dreams. License plates, house numbers, street signs, numbers on doors, on rocks, and even on people—you name it, I saw it in my dreams. Each dream would produce several numbers or number sequences. I had no idea what they meant or why I was having these crazy number dreams but I was determined to find out.

One book I picked up on the subject of numbers was Doreen Virtue's *Angel Numbers* (Hay House, 2005). It produced a complete *aha* for me, because it explained the meanings of number sequences, which, astonishingly enough, were precise answers to the challenges I was currently facing in my life. There was no doubt that they were guiding messages directing me toward my purpose. The spiritual realm was communicating with me, through numbers, that it was time for me to step onto my path.

Sparking my interest for more, I dove headlong into researching numbers on the Internet. Numerology kept coming up over and over again when I attempted to seek more information on the deeper meanings of numbers. I followed the breadcrumbs and began studying numerology, and everything began to click. I quickly picked up numbers' meanings and numerological formulas, learning the basics and then some in just a matter of weeks. In hindsight, I realized numbers were my thing—my gift and my purpose. Even as a child, I had an uncanny knack for remembering phone numbers and other series of numbers after hearing or seeing them just once. Fast-forward a few years later, I was traveling from coast to coast sharing the powerful messages and knowledge I had discovered through numbers. I was hooked, to say the least.

Everyone who took one of my courses or had a private session with me said the same thing: "You light up when you talk about numbers." It became an insatiable passion that took me deeper into my path and purpose.

Uncovering the energetic meaning of a word through the numbers came a bit later. The more I traveled and met people from different walks of life, from the average Joe to famous movie stars, the more I noticed that those who were most successful in life frequently used positive words.

Naturally, being a numbers fanatic, I analyzed everything through the numbers, so I began to delve into the world of words through the view of numbers. What I discovered was shocking. Not only did the energetic meaning of a word match its dictionary definition, it revealed even more in-depth information about how the word affected the physical world through the frequency it held. I knew this was the next chapter on my path with numbers and a message I had to share with the world.

Even after going through these amazing otherworldly experiences, I grew up to be very practical when it came to spirituality, needing a lot of facts with my faith. Yet these experiences remain the driving force in my life to accomplish my mission of showing the world that there is more than meets the eye.

Like anything based in the world of energy, an energetic pattern can be shaped and transformed depending on the other energies that interact with it. When you click off a light switch, you stop the flow of energy to that receptacle. The law of attraction is a simple spiritual or energetic rule that states "like attracts like." In other words, you attract or create in your life through the energetic frequency you send out—what you send out, you get back. The frequency or energetic vibration of a word is the missing piece in successfully applying the law of attraction to your life. The words you use can hinder or help you achieve success on any level.

You can either attract positively or negatively; when you choose to use words of a lower vibration, for example, you attract more negative energy into your life. Aligning your energy or frequency through the use of positively charged words will positively magnetize your vibration to start attracting more positive energy. When you imagine yourself driving a new sports car and feel yourself driving it, you are sending out the energetic frequency that will attract to you that sports car and you driving in it. This is how you create your reality minute by minute, whether you're aware of it or not.

The words you choose to use on a daily basis can interfere with the attraction process. Once you set the energy in motion through your vision of you driving in that sports car, your negative words can come along and flick the switch to the off position, stopping the manifesting process in its tracks. Even if the words you're using aren't directly related to the vision you want to manifest, they are still changing the energetic frequency you are sending out. You can imagine yourself driving that car all day long, but if you're going through your day using negative words or phrases like "the problem is" or "I can't," you are undermining your positive creative powers. Through the words you choose to use every day, you can be the powerful creator of the reality you were born to have.

PERCEPTION IS EVERYTHING

When it comes to the power of words, perception is everything. How we perceive a word through thought and emotion can cause it to be powerful or powerless.

I first hung out my shingle as an intuitive numerologist after having studied every book, article, and tidbit of information I could find on numerology. I didn't search out any gurus or teachers as I knew from my profound dream experiences that this had to be my journey and was to remain untainted by anyone else's views or opinions. I didn't take any of the information I was reading on blind faith; the practical side of me had to prove the validity of what I learned. Numerology came very easily to me and I found myself reading between the lines, seeing new patterns and formulas. It was as though the fabric of the universe was revealing itself to me.

I quickly started carving out my niche in the world of numbers, attracting clients with ease as they all said I had a refreshing and unique take on the numbers compared to other numerologists they had met with. I stuck with this title for some time because it fit who I was in theory, but more often than not, despite being well received by most, I felt the need to explain what that title meant. I realized it was my own perception of the word "intuitive" that created uncertainty or uneasiness. Being a very practical person, I wasn't completely comfortable shouting from the rooftop that I was psychic. I really didn't want to be envisioned as a "crystal ball psychic." In hindsight, I understand it wasn't just my uneasiness with being an intuitive, it was the fact that there was more to my path and purpose than I knew at the time. My title didn't quite feel right because it wasn't who I was truly meant to be.

As a celebrity numerologist, I've had the pleasure of traveling the country meeting thousands of interesting, successful, and famous people, revealing profound truths for them by examining their numerological makeup. It wasn't my intention in the beginning to become a celebrity numerologist. The glitz and glam of Hollywood doesn't appeal to me. What intrigues me about the celebrity sector is that they're real people with real problems, just like the rest of us, yet they serve as highly visible role models and can literally change the world with their visibility. That kind of profound change was the draw for me.

It wasn't until I had my own spiritual crisis that I finally figured out that this market was to eventually become my forte. Although I had built my platform as an intuitive numerologist and on the outside it looked like I was successful and content, on the inside I felt like I was living adjacent to my real life purpose. I knew the numbers were my gift to the world, but something was amiss and I couldn't quite put my finger on it. As the years passed, my platform continued to grow but I grew emptier inside.

My first celebrity client experience was a radio interview. I did a numerological profile for a British actor named Treva Etienne who had been in a long list of high-profile movies such as *Pirates of the Caribbean: The Curse of the Black Pearl*, *Black Hawk Down*, and *Bad Boys II*. It was my first experience with seeing firsthand that celebrities had all the same fears, concerns, and challenges as everyone else. Treva connected with me on the phone afterward and we kept in touch. It was the start of a friendship I cherish today.

Fast-forward a bit down the road to my first Hollywood red-carpet party, to which Treva's publicist had invited me. With my VIP bracelet, I danced, drank, partied like a celebrity, and even gave my business card to a few celebrities. The next day I couldn't shake the empty feeling I had. I wondered whether this was the crash celebrities feel after they come home to take off their "mask" of who people think they are.

I really admired Treva's tenacity to live in truth. Unlike much of Hollywood, he was adamant that he would never stoop below his truth level to achieve success. A pivotal conversation we had a couple of years ago stuck with me and ended up being the catalyst that helped me take the necessary steps to embrace who I was meant to be.

I confided in Treva, who is black, that my father was also black. I never really knew my father and had only met him once, but growing up in a small town with an almost entirely white population, having a black father was like a dirty little secret I protected at all costs. In my young mind, I believed it was somehow wrong to be of mixed descent. I saw firsthand, throughout my school years, the very few mixed-race children being picked on and singled out. I never did hear any child openly remark about another child's racial origins, but being an extremely perceptive and intuitive child, I came to my own conclusions and decided this was part of myself I could never truly acknowledge on any level—until I met Treva.

Treva sat me down and told me that if I was ever to be content and happy, I had to live my truth—every single piece of it. I respected his opinion and, on my plane trip home, I couldn't think of anything else. He was right, so very right, and I knew it. Embracing who I truly was on all levels, including the parts of myself I had denied all those years, was of the utmost importance. It was pivotal to my success and happiness and every fiber of my being was telling me what I had to do next.

Thankfully, my then-husband and I followed the same yearly energetic cycles (personal year cycle) and he was feeling just as restless and discontented as I was. We had hit rock bottom on a spiritual level and there was only one option—to find our truth. We took the leap and sold our house, most of our belongings, fit what we could in a five-by-eight trailer, and set out across Canada in search of ourselves. I dropped my work, my titles—everything. I was suddenly nothing and no one. I couldn't spend another day being someone who didn't feel quite right.

Sitting in the driveway of our house on closing day with nothing but our clothes and a few sentimental belongings left to our name, reality came crashing down. It was both scary and exhilarating. We had no idea who we were anymore or where we were going.

After traveling three-quarters of the way across the country, we decided to stop in Calgary, Alberta, because I had a good friend there. From the moment we arrived, synchronicity kicked into high gear and we knew we were right where we needed to be.

Within three weeks of settling in, CTV News, a national media outlet in Canada, called me out of the blue to be a guest. After the first appearance, they called me twice more within a three-month span. I still have no idea how they found me or how they even knew I was in town. From there it was a snowball effect; more media appearances, a flurry of celebrity clients, and coincidental connections with all the right people that propelled me fast and hard into the numbers again, taking me to new heights.

But this time it was different. I had stepped back into the numerologist role but had yet to fully embrace my old title. This was an opportunity to reinvent and rebrand myself in alignment with my truth. Knowing I wanted to continue to work the numbers and work with celebrities because of their ability to affect others on a broad scale, the choice was clear: I was a celebrity numerologist. Not only that, but at this point I had earned the title of "celebrity" in my own right. For the first time in my life, I could stand tall in this new image of myself, knowing this was my truth and who I was meant to be. No longer did I have to explain myself or try to convince someone to believe in me. Most importantly, for the first time in my life, I had no secrets to hide. I finally embraced myself in my totality.

That one-word change—intuitive to celebrity—made all the difference on an inner and outer level and has changed the trajectory of my life. I now have clients from major movies and TV shows such as the Twilight Saga's *Breaking Dawn*, *The Big Bang Theory*, and *Pirates of the Caribbean: The Curse of the Black Pearl*; I also work with a Hollywood stylist, a celebrity judge, and an NBC director. I'm considered an expert in my field, a regular and sought-after guest on national media outlets. I also own the rapidly growing online radio and TV network Authentic You Media.

I share this not to brag, but to show that the power you put behind a word can assist you in manifesting your dreams. A word has to resonate with you and be in alignment with what is true to you in order to manifest what you desire. Like my own example highlights, this is particularly true when it comes to who you believe you are.

In the more than ten years I've been working with the numbers, I have had the privilege of helping guide the lives of thousands of people from all walks of life. I don't take lightly the honor and responsibility of assisting in the shaping of decisions and choices that not only mold an individual's destiny but ultimately our global destiny. One of the main reasons I fell in love with numerology as a branch of the metaphysical is that it is a mathematical science. The level of accuracy is unmatched compared to other branches of metaphysics like astrology, tarot, and the like. When you work with numbers, there are no gray areas. In numerology, a number either matches an energetic pattern or it doesn't.

I firmly believe that there are deeper truths we are all meant to know and our soul is constantly guiding us to them. It is in following the signs from the unseen spirit world (or breadcrumbs, as I like to call them) that we can navigate toward and reveal those truths.

This book is a breadcrumb for you to follow. Read it from cover to cover and follow its contents to peel back a layer masking your own truth. Words are powerful creative energies that can change your world in an instant. Language is a gift unique to humans; it is meant to serve as a tool in your journey.

You now have in your hands a handbook to harness the vibration of language and transform your life. *The Energy of Words: Use the Vibration of Language to Manifest the Life You Desire* takes you through the steps to discover your personal jargon list, helping you pinpoint exactly what you're manifesting in your life through the words you choose to use. Your Top Ten Positive Power Words are the key to transforming your life from negative to positive. These are your ten most frequently used words; these words carry the most energetic weight, and changing them to reflect what you really want can quickly and profoundly shift your life and perspective. What words are you creating with?

Choose well, choose wisely, and choose positively!

CHAPTER 1

The Gift of Language and Your Conscious Choice for Change

What is it about a word that has the ability to strike a chord within? Just a single word can instantly melt our heart, infuse us with anger, or completely change our perspective. Most of us take words for granted, because after all, they're just words—right?

Regardless of the language we speak, words connect us on a far deeper level than just getting our point across. Each word carries its own energetic vibration and can have a profound impact on the quality of our lives. The gift of language allows us to become active creators from the moment we utter our first word.

When a child transitions from vocalizing sounds to speaking words, it is a celebrated event. More than just a developmental milestone, it marks the day when a child enters the realm of conscious creation. Conscious choice replaces natural instincts, and the child begins the journey of creating his or her destiny.

Many of us are familiar with the law of attraction, which states "like attracts like"; in other words, what we think about we bring about (positive or negative). Although this law works when correctly and consistently applied, it can be tricky business keeping our focus on what we desire 100 percent of the time (we're only human). Doubt often sets in and we begin to fall back into negative thought and speech patterns, undermining our attempts to make positive changes. The important word here is *patterns*. As creatures of habit, examining and changing our negative patterns is the key to unlocking our full manifestation power. Thinking about what we want is only half the equation; changing our autopilot language program is the missing variable.

We think, speak, and write using words, yet these seemingly neutral forms are actually the building blocks of our lives. Language is undeniably a gift and, as the only species to have this tool available to us, we have a responsibility to use it consciously. Words afford us the ability to have a proactive role in the creation and progression of our lives. Imagine a world where language suddenly became obsolete—talk about being at a loss for words!

THE LAW OF ATTRACTION

The essence of this book is written around the law of attraction, meaning that what you send out to the universe through thoughts and intentions, you attract back to you. For example, if you practice being optimistic and send out positive energy in any form, you attract more positive energy to you. Likewise, if you're more of a pessimist and send out negative energy, you attract more negative energy. This includes the thoughts and intentions you put behind the words you use, because many of our thoughts are word-based, not just imagery.

Steve Pavlina, author of *Personal Development for Smart People* and over one thousand articles on personal growth and development, has a life story that perfectly exemplifies successful application of the law of attraction. He hasn't had a "real" job since 1992 and enjoys living his passion. Sounds like he has it all together, but it wasn't always that way for him. His journey is an extreme one. He went from sitting in a jail cell facing felony charges to becoming a globally recognized author, speaker, and personal-growth expert. How did he accomplish such a feat? Solely through changing his thinking patterns.

Given his incredible backstory, Pavlina has obviously learned a lot about the law of attraction and the power of choice. The best part about life is that we all have choice as the driving force behind our ability to create. Once you become conscious of the fact that your life is based completely on the choices you make, you can begin to shift your focus toward making the right choices that make you feel good—thus, creating the life you desire. The power is in your hands.

If you're feeling powerless to make changes in your life for any reason, it's a choice you're making for yourself. You are feeling powerless because this is the conscious choice you decided upon. By labeling yourself and believing that you are powerless,

you attract situations, people, and things into your awareness
that bring about a sense of a loss of power to change.

Steve Pavlina does a great job of simplifying the law of attraction and its relationship to our power of choice:

> When you assume 100 percent responsibility for every-
> thing you're experiencing in your reality right now—ab-
> solutely everything—then you assume the power
> to alter your reality by rechanneling your thoughts.
>
> This entire reality is your creation. Feel good about
> that. Feel grateful for the richness of your world. And
> then begin creating the reality you truly want by mak-
> ing decisions and holding intentions. Think about what
> you desire, and withdraw your thoughts from what you
> don't want. The most natural, easiest way to do this is
> to pay attention to your emotions. Thinking about your
> desires feels good, and thinking about what you don't
> want makes you feel bad. When you notice yourself
> feeling bad, you've caught yourself thinking about some-
> thing you don't want. Turn your focus back towards
> what you do want, and your emotional state will im-
> prove rapidly. As you do this repeatedly, you'll begin to
> see your physical reality shift too, first in subtle ways
> and then in bigger leaps.

As you can see, the keyword here is "choice," but the feelings
(emotions) we have about that choice provide it with fuel
(whether positive or negative) to affect our lives.

As with anything you choose, the way you feel about the words you decide to include in your vocabulary every day—in your thought processes, speech patterns, or written expressions—shapes the way they will affect your life. In this book, much emphasis is placed on how you feel about the words you're using and whether they make you feel good or not. If you're still uncertain about how to successfully apply the law of attraction in your life, the easiest way to stay focused with it is to check your emotions. Do you feel good about your decisions? If so, then you're on the right track. If not, choose again until it does feel good.

Below is a great example from Roi Solberg, an intuitive. Roi's story highlights what it means to manifest through the words you choose to use and that a single word can shift your perspective on any situation:

New adventures beyond my comfort zone were scary. I never let it stop me—I'd put them at the top of my list and do first, but with fear and trepidation.

That all changed when I realized that accomplishing things through fear created more situations for me to experience fear. When I shifted to affirming trust, well, major changes took place.

My experiences are now more fulfilling because I trust everything will work out for my higher good.

Now, new adventures are easy peasy and filled with an abundance of trust.

In Roi's example, switching from the self-doubting, self-critical, indecisive energy of the word "fear" to the confident, assured, and doubtlessness of the word "trust" made all the difference in terms of manifesting more contentment and certainty in her life.

THE BASICS OF LANGUAGE

Although the origins of language remain obscure, recent studies show there are about six thousand languages in use today[4] (a third of them in Africa). That's a lot of words. It is theorized by some that all of those languages in existence today were derived from a single language only fifty thousand to seventy thousand years ago.[5] Considering that language is relatively new, it is no coincidence that the world has evolved substantially, like no other time in history, during the last thousand years.

Words are unique to humans. Animals rely on instinctual tones to communicate, but humans have an elaborate communication repertoire to drawn upon. Our communication ability comes from a special center in the brain called the cortical speech center or the Broca's area, discovered by the French neurosurgeon, Paul Broca, which operates not on an instinctual basis but a rational one.[6] In simple terms, we're able to think before we speak and can therefore choose the words we utter.

Arguably, over 90 percent of our communication is done through nonverbal means. While this may be true, take note of what is going on in the background the next time you're communicating nonverbally. No doubt you'll find a wordy conversation happening in your mind.

No matter how you look at it, language is an integral piece of the human existence. Words have both built and destroyed nations and continue to profoundly shape and shift our planet. Miscommunication and misinterpretation of language has been the start and end of many things both big and small, from wars to lovers' quarrels. Words can be the ultimate healing tool or a weapon of mass destruction.

The Bible is an incredible example of how the interpretation of language can profoundly shift the meaning of a word. Some believe the scriptures are purely metaphorical while some take a literal approach to the Bible's teachings. This is also true for other spiritual texts in many cultures. Our world would be vastly different today if words were not open to individual interpretation and perception. Perception is truly in the eye of the beholder.

Each of us is a micro of the macro, and therefore the energy we're sending out via the words we choose to use has a ripple effect. Consciously choosing positively charged words will help you make a positive shift in your own life, but keep in mind that your words will also have a positive impact on the world around you. Who says one person can't change the world?

Whether your native tongue is English, Hebrew, Spanish, or sign language, the words you use are constantly shaping your world. In our youth, through both verbal and nonverbal cues, we learn the meaning of thousands of words. We not only integrate the straightforward definition, but we also assign feelings associated with words based on our personal experiences involving those words. The feelings we hold about something have a great deal to do with how we perceive it, and our perception is precisely how we shape our reality.

Although perception is a choice we make based mainly on a combination of observing and drawing upon accumulated knowledge and past personal experiences, there are other underlying factors that may be swaying us one way or the other. Some factors may be carved into our DNA and are ancient in origin.

A study done in 2005 by Robert Schrauf, associate professor of applied linguistics and anthropologist at Pennsylvania State University, revealed that negative words dominate our vocabulary. The study (titled appropriately), "Negative Words Dominate Language," showed that all groups in the study, regardless of age or nationality, had the same results: "Half of all the words that people produce from their working vocabulary to express emotion are negative. And 30 percent are positive and 20 percent neutral," says Schrauf.[7]

The study results intrigued Schrauf so much that he began to dig a little deeper. His research uncovered even more negativity. Interestingly, there are five to seven basic emotions that show up in every language and appear to have similar meanings. Among thirty-seven languages, the words for joy, fear, anger, sadness, disgust, shame, and guilt each carry very similar definitions.

If you haven't noticed already, the list of universally shared words above are all negative except one. Shocking, isn't it? Why are we so negative? Further evidence reveals it may be a coping mechanism. Our survival depends on being able to express ourselves correctly and precisely in the case that something is causing us pain, suffering, or is jeopardizing our survival or quality of life. A wider variety of negative words to choose from appears to have developed from necessity and has a more primal basis.

An article titled "Negative Words Dominate Language" by Lee Dye, a columnist on ABCNews.com, highlights a quote from Schrauf indicating that more mental processing is required of us when thinking and speaking negative words:

> Negative words, like fear or anger, signal a threat or a danger. There's a tendency to slow down our processing or think more carefully. While positive emotions tend to tell us that things are benign or safe or everything is OK. So processing of those emotions is more script-like. Things are going OK, things are proceeding according to the outline of my life, so you don't do a lot of word processing.[8]

Again, it boils down to our instincts. The word "fear" indicates a threat to our survival, so we therefore pay more attention to this word and the mental processing behind it. Positive words require less mental attention because there's no threatening trigger associated with them. Positive and neutral words are processed in an "autopilot" mode.

Could it be that we tend to dwell more often on the negative than positive merely because we're instinctually spending more time processing and focusing on negative words? If we spend more time thinking about negative words, based on the law of attraction, negativity would tip the scales to bring the focus of our attention on the negative things and therefore we manifest more of the same. Sounds like a cycle that could be hard to break.

DECIDING TO CHANGE

Instinctual response is innate and determined by the "hard-wiring" of the nervous system. It is usually inflexible, a given stimulus triggering a given response.[9] Reflexes are an example of an instinctual behavior. Alternatively, a learned behavior or a habit is formed through repeated experiences. During our early days as humans, we were almost purely operating on instinct. Now that we have evolved to become more conscious creatures, we understand that we have a choice in everything we say or do. Instinct is not nearly as much a daily factor in our lives anymore, since we don't have the daily threats to our survival that our ancestors did, yet the automatic response still remains a part of our hardwiring.

So the question remains: How do we undo millions of years' worth of habitual behavior? The answer is simple: conscious choice. As human beings, we're poised to take the reins of our creative power and begin to consciously choose the life we dwell in. We have always had the ability to create any reality we choose, but it has not been until now that we have recognized this ability. Unfortunately, even though we now have the ability to recognize our power of choice, it's easier to fall back on instinct and old patterns of existence. Conscious choice is a relatively new option available to us at this point in our evolutionary journey, so it only stands to reason that it's going to take some practice to get it into a habitual behavior.

As you delve deeper into this book, you'll realize there's no easy fix for manifesting the life you desire. Old habits tend to have a firm grasp and it takes time, patience, and effort to change them. Thankfully, you've got the lesson plan literally in the palm of your hand. You may be hardwired to put more focus and attention on the negative, but you're about to be given the tools you need to rearrange the wiring and give your life a positive charge.

Language is truly a gift but its exact origins are still unknown. Could it be that the electrical pathways we developed in order to be able to process words may have led us to the ability to consciously choose? Was language the precursor to conscious choice? Regardless of how or why language came to be, there is no denying that the words we use are the missing link to manifesting our reality moment by moment. Through the power of words, you can take your life from chaos to clarity by becoming the conscious creator you were destined to be. The choice is yours.

ANGELIC WORD POWER

C. J. is another example of an individual who had a profound angelic experience, a perfect example of the human ability to make conscious choices:

> After my husband and I had moved in together in the early years, something unexpected happened. I began

experiencing with vivid detail all the previous negative moments in my life. It was like reliving all my traumatic experiences one by one. Each memory was endowed with an intensity that I cannot describe fully. I became despondent and literally stuck in the past.

When my mind fell apart, I not only became depressed, but very angry. I couldn't understand why I was falling apart when things were actually going in a positive direction. It seemed like the ultimate irony. Here I had someone who loved me for me, yet I was miserable and couldn't seem to enjoy it. This went on for over three months before an incredible thing happened.

One evening, I was going through my usual nighttime routine getting ready for bed. Emotionally, I felt bruised and blue from head to toe. I thought that my situation would be a never-ending one. I was alone in the room but starting speaking out loud to no one in particular.

"I'm so tired of hurting. I just can't do this anymore. Why is this happening to me?"

The room was silent. No answer came.

"I feel so alone. I feel like nothing matters. Why do I feel this way?"

The room was still silent. No answer came.

"Someone take this pain from me. I'm tired of hurting."

Then I heard a soft clear voice. A singular idea came across from the air around me.

"You're not hurting."

"What do you mean, not hurting!" I said angrily to the voice.

"You're not hurting."

I sat in silence for several moments. Then I heard the voice again, so clearly. It was like another person was sitting next to me. At the time, hearing the voice come from seemingly no one didn't really alarm me.

"You're not hurting. You are healing."

I considered what I had heard very carefully. "Healing" was a word that had never entered my consciousness in regard to this situation. I tried healing on for size. I thought about what it meant to be healing instead of hurting. What if the voice were right?

I spoke again: "If I'm healing then I can't do it alone." At that very moment, I raised my hands toward the ceiling inviting anyone who might help me. What happened next was the most tangible spiritual experience I've ever known. Anything that had happened in my childhood paled by comparison. What was conveyed to me in milliseconds was unlike anything I had ever felt before. I was tingly from head to toe. It was the consummate spiritual experience in one enormous flash of light. I felt the room fill up all around me with an intense love—pure and unconditional. And then I saw where the voice had come from. Standing around me in my bedroom was a whole group of breathtaking angels. I was speechless.

At that moment, everything became instantly clear. I could easily see the distinction between using the word "healing" instead of "hurting." I fully knew what it had felt like to be in a state of hurting, so I tried to imagine what healing would be like. While looking at everything as an experience of healing, my perception shifted effortlessly from one of utter pain to one of hopeful reflection.

A calm filled my entire body. I relaxed for the first time in months. Healing was doable because I could see healing as a process and that I was taking part in it instead of endless suffering I could see would have no end.

I call that day my awakening. Using the word "healing" to describe my situation entered my consciousness that day and set me free. I realized that my perception of the situation had kept me stuck in a hopeless place. My perception had been the key to everything.

In C. J.'s case, making the shift from living through the lens of the word "hurting" to the word "healing" was paramount. Instead of manifesting more hurt-filled experiences and going around in a circle of unhappiness and suffering, she chose to step into the frequency of healing, thus transforming what she was manifesting in her life into what she truly desired for herself and her family.

In chapter 3, we'll go through the steps to convert a word to numerical form using numerology. We'll dig deeper into what a word means from an energetic standpoint. To whet your appetite, let's briefly examine what these two words mean for C. J.'s manifesting power. The word "hurting" is a 7 frequency; in the negative, the number 7 has the traits of distrust, skepticism, and isolation. The word "healing" has a 2 energetic frequency; 2 is the number of intuition, sensitivity, balance, harmony, and cooperation. Based on the number meanings of these two words, it's clear how and why the switch had such a profound impact on how C. J. viewed her situation.

CHAPTER 2

The Progression and Forms of Communication

When we think about language and its expression, we automatically think of speaking and writing. However, we actually express language in three forms: thought, speech, and the written word. We often forget that before we speak or write language, we also think about it. By far, the most forgotten form of language is in fact the most powerful—the language in our thoughts. The words running through our head on a daily basis are constantly shaping our reality in a multitude of ways.

THE BASICS OF HOW WE THINK IN WORDS

As children, usually in the first two years of life, we begin to express our thoughts and emotions through language. Until that point, there is a tremendous amount of behind-the-scenes learning going on in the form of thought. At the tender age of two, a child's language skills on the thought level are much more advanced than they could ever express verbally. They understand hundreds if not thousands of words, yet they can only verbally utter a fraction of them. The mind is a powerful tool and can process and assimilate words far faster than we can express them verbally. What does this say about the power of words in thought form? A thought is worth a thousand spoken words!

Think about the last time you did any kind of public speaking, such as giving a toast at a wedding reception, doing a presentation at school, or even going to a job interview. Most of us are familiar with the enormous amount of thought that goes behind any of those nerve-wracking experiences. If you're like the majority of the population, you tend to run through the entire verbal scenario in your mind many times before the big day arrives.

According to the law of attraction, what we think about, we bring about. Focusing all your thought processes on the possible "what if" scenarios before a big job interview usually makes the "what if" scenarios manifest in some form or another, no matter how long you spent perfecting your answers. You can't blame it on bad luck—it's the power of thought at work.

There's always a running commentary in our minds, and words outweigh our thought processes over imagery. We may envision ourselves acing the job interview, but the voiceover behind that mental scene could be painting a different picture altogether. According to a widely quoted National Science Foundation study, on average we process up to sixty thousand thoughts per day, which is more than we could ever express verbally.[10] It depends on the person how many of these thoughts are positive or negative, but the great news is that you have control over which one is more dominant. You can instantly and drastically change your life for the better just by catching yourself in the act of negative mental chatter and shifting it into the positive. Talk about serious mind control!

Speech and Writing

Now that you know the basics of how we think in words and the effects it can have on our day-to-day life, let's examine the two most commonly known forms of language: speech and writing.

Verbal communication has been around since the time of the cavemen, but in only the last few thousand years have those verbal sounds been expressed in the form of words or language. No scientist has been able to pinpoint the exact date of the creation of language, but science is in agreement that it is a relatively new form of expression. Writing has been around since the cavemen days in the form of illustrations and symbols, but the written word is a newer form of expression.

It's no surprise that we've witnessed an explosion in terms of the progress of civilization around the same time language entered the scene. Taken at face value, we can safely assume language lessened misunderstandings and miscommunications, allowing ideas to be exchanged and acted upon readily and easily. But what about our personal creative power that was achieved when we could apply words and meanings to everything in life? With language came the gift of becoming the creator of our own reality.

Some of us express ourselves better through speech and others through writing, but both are powerful. When we read a love letter or hear our favorite love song, each has the potential to move us emotionally. It is the vibration of the words—not the method of delivery—that affects us on an energetic level.

Whether we think, speak, or write a word, its vibration never changes. Theoretically, a word has the same impact on our energy regardless of how it is expressed—or does it? What if we said verbally to our partner "I love you" versus writing it on a piece of paper? Obviously the effects of the verbally expressed love would be more powerful because we're able to add in body language, tone of voice, and other cues that add to the energetic effect of those three words. As humans, we are also visual beings; our experience is constantly being shaped by our perception.

Thought

Which form of language is most powerful? Which one do we focus on first to begin shifting our lives from negative to positive? Although it's clear that the spoken word can be much more energetically profound in a social situation, when it comes to our personal inner evolution, words in the form of thought are by far our most prized life-transforming tool.

From an energetic perspective, words in the form of thought affect us first. This is because we process many more thoughts in the form of words per day than we speak, but also because thoughts originate within us and have a ripple effect outward in our reality. For example, if a repeating thought you hold is "I'm not worth it," then it isn't long before others start treating you poorly, too. Based on the scientific definition of the law of attraction, we attract people, places, things, and situations that bring about experiences matching the same frequency at which we are vibrating, just like atoms that are polarized as positive or negative. If you are sending out negative thoughts and feelings that you are unworthy, you will experience a reality where you are unworthy.

The spoken word affects those around you more directly because, unless they're telepathic, others can't hear what you're thinking. If you say to someone "I hate you," your hate-filled frequency is immediately permeating their energetic field with a negative vibration. The written word resides somewhere in between the two. When we write something, there is so much room for interpretation by the reader that it is the least predictable of all three forms of language in terms of how it will affect us. Whether we write a letter to our child or a resignation letter to a difficult boss, there is an undertone of feeling that goes into every word through the choice and phrasing of the words used. One person may read paragraph of words and get a totally different meaning or feeling than another. It certainly brings new meaning to "reading between the lines."

We're in the midst of the technological age where more and more of our language expression is nonverbal. Texts, e-mails, and the Internet are edging us toward a society dominated by the written word. Language is evolving, and it is no coincidence that this is happening now. There is a more positive overtone to becoming less verbally outspoken now; as a result, many of us have recognized our most powerful manifestation tool is thought. Is the move to a less verbally outspoken society a natural progression? Does it indicate that we are evolving on a soul level, becoming more aligned with the spiritual self that communicates nonverbally? The answer is *yes*.

The future of the expression of language is to continue to move away from the spoken word, tipping the scales toward a world where writing is the primary means of communication.

The good news is that it takes more conscious thought to write than it does to speak words. The techno age really doesn't have to destroy the brains of our teens after all. All jokes aside, what this means for us globally is that we are now putting more thought and energy into our language expression. Not everyone is using this expression positively—yet. Viewed from a broader perspective, we are in the primitive stages of transitioning from predominately verbal to nonverbal communication. At the moment, most of it is instinctual and physical (or ego-based), but we are in the learning stages. As we move deeper into this shift away from the spoken word, we will begin to see the written word being used more positively on a regular basis. Mindless texts and chatroom banter will pave the way for a much deeper communication connection between souls. We must learn to walk before we can run.

CHAPTER 3

Determining the Vibration of a Word through the Language of Numbers

WHAT IS ENERGY?

In the eyes of the scientific community, the widely accepted and quoted definition of energy is "the capacity of a physical system to perform work".s Based on this definition, there are two main forms of energy: kinetic energy and potential energy. These two categories of energy represent what many of us think of when we hear the word "energy." Electricity, moving water, a windmill, and a battery cell are all forms of the two main types of energy as seen through the eyes of traditional science.

From a metaphysical vantage point, since Einstein discovered the relativity theory, it has been accepted that matter is a form of energy. Energy is made up of molecules rotating or vibrating at various rates of speed. In the physical world, molecules rotate at a very slow and constant rate, causing the physical world to appear solid. The slower the speed, the more dense or solid the matter appears to be. In the metaphysical or spiritual world or ethereal dimension—where things are freer and less dense—the molecules vibrate at a much faster rate of speed. To the average person, a word is merely an inanimate thing that we use to communicate with others; most of the time, we're completely unaware that the words we choose are constantly and continually shaping our existence every time we use them because they are also energy: energetic frequencies or patterns.

Language has fascinated mankind for centuries and many have attempted to shine a light on its secrets. In recent years, words have taken on new meaning with the popularity of the law of attraction, which says, "What you think about, you bring about." There is a trend toward becoming much more conscious of the words we use and how we use them, but we're still flying blind. Using words at face value (definition only) is like taking a pill because it looks tasty even though we have no idea what it will do to us. We need to know what that pill (or word) is made of and how it will affect us.

Even if you've never heard of the law of attraction before, knowing which words resonate with you on an energetic level can assist you in pinpointing destructive vocabulary. This alone can quickly shift your life into the positive.

Science has taught us that energy vibrates and follows patterns. It can be molded, redirected, converted, and transformed. As an intangible force, there is endless creative potential in the realm of energy because it takes many forms. In a world where the building blocks of life are made of energy, words carry their own unique energetic patterns and vibrations. We are constantly shaping our reality with the energetic vibration of the words we speak, think, and write.

The old childhood rhyme "stick and stones may break my bones, but words will never hurt me" is a good representation of society's belief that words are just words. Knowing the vibration of a word gives us the power to understand the impact it has on us. Is your everyday jargon more like an artist's gentle sculpting tools or weapons of mass destruction? Let's find out!

THE THREE PLANES OF EXISTENCE

Before we go deeper into the vibration of a word, it is first necessary to look at the three planes of existence here on Earth to clarify how a word might affect both our inner and outer world. The New Age and metaphysical communities believe that we are spiritual beings in a physical body and have three levels through which we operate or express with our physical form. These are the mind plane, the soul plane, and the physical plane.

The mind plane encompasses our intellectual processes like thought, creativity, dreams, phobias or fears, imagination, and memory. Words that work through or trigger the mind-plane faculties are some of the most powerful words, as thought is the primary tool used in creating and shaping goals, dreams, and desires.

The soul plane includes both the emotional and spiritual activities within your being. Love, hate, anger, rage, passion, lust, bliss, and peace are just some of the feeling sensations processed through the soul plane. Operating within the boundaries of the soul plane allows you to put emotions behind your desires to accelerate and heighten your manifesting powers. Words that trigger or touch the soul plane energies are just as powerful as the words working with the mind plane. The emotional and soulful energies are the fuel in your manifestation engine, fueling the thoughts you begin with on the mind plane.

In order for a word to have manifestation power in our lives, we must give it power through thought and feeling. When a young child says a profane word, it usually remains neutral because the child is likely unaware of the word's definition. When an adult speaks a negative word, it can have all sorts of feelings behind it, such as anger, guilt, or fear, depending on the speaker's experiences. Knowing both the dictionary meaning of a word and its vibrational definition can show you precisely what you're manifesting through the power of words.

The third level of existence is the physical plane. Believe it or not, despite it being the most tangible, it is the least powerful in terms of manifesting your reality. This is considered the "doing" plane, enveloping all of your physical sensations like touch, smell, hearing, taste, sight, physical pain, sensuality, and more. Most words that activate physical sensory stimulation are first processed through the mind plane and soul plane.

Now that you're familiar with the way that the unseen world of energy operates within the three planes of existence, let's move on to how energy can be represented through the vibration and definition of the universal language of numbers.

DECODING THE LANGUAGE OF ENERGY THROUGH NUMBERS

Imagine words as melodies you sing and each letter as a note. When we hear an upbeat song on the radio, it can change our mood and set the tone of our day. The words we think, speak, and write are all parts of our personal theme song. Is your song a down-on-your-luck country tune, a bubbly pop track, or somewhere between?

A word's dictionary meaning is only half of its definition. The other half lies within the vibrational meaning of a word, which can be measured using numbers. When music is sung from a sheet of musical notes, the music is deciphered from the codes on the sheet. Numbers are another kind of code that can be used to decipher the energetic meaning of a word.

By applying the universal language of numbers, we can convert any word to its energetic form. Everything in the world can be measured, sorted, or counted using numbers. Like words, numbers also have their own unique energetic signature. All numbers in existence are created using the base numbers 1–9 (and 0, which is a symbol rather than a number).

As previously stated, Pythagoras discovered through his study of numbers that all things are based in numbers. He said, "Everything lies veiled in numbers." In his Mystery School, he taught this concept, but his findings were so astonishing that he swore his students to secrecy. The Pythagorean

Society took an active part in politics, which unfortunately led to the demise of the Mystery School and its following as the government did not approve of such a secret order[11]. The school and meeting places were burned along with much of the knowledge and information contained within them. However, thanks to the revelations of this Greek genius, we now possess the tools necessary to allow us to harness the vibration of language.

Based on Pythagoras's findings, every number in existence is created from the base numbers 1–9, which are the numerical figures that form the basis of numerology. Drawing upon the theory that all things are energy at their core, numbers are also energy and can represent the energy patterns within and around us. Think of numbers as spiritual DNA. Anything in the world can be reduced to a base number or energetic frequency of 1–9 and this number code can tell you the spiritual or energetic essence of a person, place, or thing based on the number's definition.

We're about to dive headlong into the process of uncovering the energetic meaning of all the words you use in your daily life, but before we do that, let's look at a snapshot of some of the more popular positive and negative words and what they mean. Rewriting your vocabulary list is easy when you know what you're actually saying.

The word "hate," for example, is a harsh word by the dictionary definition and the vibrational meaning is "distrust." If the word "hate" is thought, spoken, or written, it packs a powerful punch in a very negative way.

The word "believe" is an inspirational word that energetically means "freedom of expression."

The word "can't" is a submissive word with a vibrational meaning of "codependent."

The word "problem" is a skeptical word that subliminally says "pessimistic" and "judgmental." A common phrase we're all guilty of using at some point: "But the problem is ..." Using "problem" in this way creates a problem before there is one; it creates pessimistic and judgmental energy the moment the word is uttered.

CONVERTING WORDS TO NUMBERS

The process of assigning numerical values to letters or words is not based in numerology alone. Many cultures and traditions have used similar methods to convert words to numerical meanings and values for centuries. The Jewish tradition has a system of assigning esoteric meaning to words based on their numerical values; this is called *gematria*. Converting letters to numerical form, as seen in current numerology systems, is also based on this Jewish practice of gematria:

Hebrew Gematria Chart [13]

	א	ב	ג	ד	ה	ו	ז	ח	ט
Name	Alef	Bet	Gimel	Dalet	He	Vav	Zayen	Het	Tet
Absolute Value	1	2	3	4	5	6	7	8	9
Ordinal Value	1	2	3	4	5	6	7	8	9
Reduced Value	1	2	3	4	5	6	7	8	9

	י	כ	ל	מ	נ	ס	ע	פ	צ
Name	Yod	Kaf	Lamed	Mem	Nun	Samekh	Ayin	Pe	Tsadi
Absolute Value	10	20	30	40	50	60	70	80	90
Ordinal Value	10	11	12	13	14	15	16	17	18
Reduced Value	1	2	3	4	5	6	7	8	9

	ק	ר	ש	ת	ך	ם	ן	ף	ץ
Name	Qof	Resh	Shin	Tav	Final Kaf	Final Mem	Final Nun	Final Pe	Final Tsadi
Absolute Value	100	200	300	400	500	600	700	800	900
Ordinal Value	19	20	21	22	23	24	25	26	27
Reduced Value	1	2	3	4	5	6	7	8	9

Gematria is a system of calculating numerical value to a word or phrase in the belief that words or phrases with identical numerical values bear some relation to each other, or bear some relation to the number. Hidden meanings and words can be found by using values of the underlying letters (see chart). A good Gematria example is the Hebrew word Chai ("life"), which is composed of two letters which add up to 18. This has made 18 a "lucky number" among Jews, and gifts in multiples of $18 are very common.[12]

The diagram on the previous page is a gematria word conversion chart. Like Pythagorean numerology, its foundation is constructed of nine base numbers used in converting letters and words to numbers.

Although Pythagoras was considered the father of numerology, his work related more to numbers as symbols. His theories were based on his insights that everything progressed in predictable cycles, and he assumed a similar connection to the alphabet. His work provided the basis of what is now called numerology.

Modern numerology has various antecedents. Ruth A. Drayer's book, *Numerology: The Power in Numbers* (Square One, 2002) says that around the turn of the century (from 1800 to 1900 CE), Mrs. L. Dow Balliett combined Pythagoras's work with biblical reference. In the mid-1970s, Balliett's student, Dr. Juno Jordan, changed numerology further and helped it to become the system known today under the title "Pythagorean."

Jordan combined Pythagoras's initial work of the vibration of numbers with Balliett's work with biblical references to form what is now known as the Pythagorean Numerology System.[14]

The diagram below is the Pythagorean word-conversion chart based on the Latin alphabet (more will be discussed in chapter 10 on how to convert words in other languages). Each letter in the alphabet is assigned a number from 1–9, starting with the first letter and labeling sequentially until 9 is reached. Once you move through all 9 numbers, you return to 1 again and continue matching letters to numbers, like this: A = 1, B = 2, C = 3, D = 4, E = 5, F = 6, G = 7, H = 8, I = 9, J = 1, and so on, until you reach the end of the alphabet. This is the standard chart used in numerology today. (Be sure to mark this page for easy reference when you begin your journey into your own word conversions!)

Word Conversion Chart								
1	2	3	4	5	6	7	8	9
A	B	C	D	E	F	G	H	I
J	K	L	M	N	O	P	Q	R
S	T	U	V	W	X	Y	Z	

Now that you have an understanding of the history and meaning of numerology and its relation to numbers and letters, let's go further into the world of energy as it relates to number vibrations and the true meaning of a word.

Whether you're converting verbs, nouns, adjectives, or names, you'll find as I have that the accuracy of this chart is impeccable. In my practice over the years, I have used it for many things, including helping clients pick a suitable business name or stage name to ensure success; assisting with a move by determining the vibration of a city, country, or street name and how it relates to the individual's energetic makeup; and even helping to name children.

One of my most memorable experiences as a numerologist was to assist a mother in the naming process of her six-week-old son. This mother was having a difficult time deciding on a name for her boy, and she felt guilty that he had yet to be named at a month and a half old. After converting all of her name choices to their numerical meaning, I gave my opinion of which name would be optimal for her son based on the name vibrations and comparing them with the energies he carried in his date of birth. She confirmed with me afterward that I had suggested the very name she felt was the right one all along. This experience was one of many that have reaffirmed for me the power behind the numbers and their relation to all things, including words.

Let's put the chart into action by decoding the word "live." What does it mean to really live? After converting the letters to numerical values, it looks like this: L = 3, I = 9, V = 4, E = 5.

The next step is to add the numbers to get the main energetic pattern of the word. Imagine each number value as a neutron or electron and the sum as the entire atom. The sum of a word's numerical value shows you precisely what you're creating with that word's vibration. Here are the numerical values of the letters in the word "live" written as an addition equation:

$3 + 9 + 4 + 5 = 21$

If you arrive at a double-digit answer, reduce again to get the overall energetic pattern as a single digit. Remember, all numbers are created using the base numbers 1–9 (and 0), therefore we must reduce to a single-digit number to find the base value. The sum we arrived at above is 21 and it is reduced like this:

$2 + 1 = 3$

The base pattern of the word "live" is 3.

At the end of this chapter, you'll find the base number meanings of 1–9. You'll see that there are both positive and negative traits of each number. How you use a word will decide which traits you'll need to focus on changing. For example, if you use the word "live" in the phrase "I don't want to live like this anymore," the vibration of that word is being used negatively and the negative qualities of the 3 apply. The negative qualities of 3, such as critical and self-doubting, are dominating the word's vibration. Alternatively, using "live" in a positive phrase like "I want to live like there's no tomorrow" draws on the positive qualities of the 3, such as inspiration and imagination.

The word "problem" is another example of a word that is frequently used negatively and is often responsible for being a hindrance in otherwise happy lives. If you convert "problem" to numerical values, it looks like this: P = 7, R = 9, O = 6, B = 2, L = 3, E = 5, M = 4.

The sum of those digits is $7 + 9 + 6 + 2 + 3 + 5 + 4 = 36$. In reducing 36, we come to a single digit of 9: $3 + 6 = 9$. The word "problem" vibrates to the number 9 energy.

This is a terrific example of how words can be both positive and negative. Flipping back to the definitions at the end of the chapter, we see that 9 is the "idealistic humanitarian." Humanitarian energy wants nothing more than to fix problems, but most of us use the word "problem" in a negative way. When we start phrases with "the problem is," we're drawing upon the negative qualities of the 9, such as opinionated and judgmental. Alternatively, responding with "no problem!" sends the energy into the positive.

The word "hate" is a strong word by the dictionary definition, and the vibrational meaning is "distrust." Converting it to numerical values, H = 8, A = 1, T = 2, E = 5, we come to the base sum of 8 + 1 + 2 + 5 = 16. Converting to a single digit: 1 + 6 = 7. The number 7 is the truth-seeker number; in the negative, it is a very distrusting and skeptical energy. If the word "hate" is thought, spoken, or written, it packs a powerful punch in a very negative way. When we speak or are spoken to using the word "hate," we feel violated or stripped of our power. As the number of truth, 7 is harsh and raw in the negative form.

As you can see, the power in a word is all in how you use it. Language is a powerful manifesting tool, and like any tool, you need to know how to use it properly to achieve the results you want. Words are the missing piece in the law of attraction. Imagining what we want and holding that vision is only a part of the process in manifesting the life we desire. Like attracts like, and if you're going through your day ejecting negative word vibrations out into your energetic surroundings, you will attract more negative energy. If your sights are set on a gorgeous house in the hills but several times a day you catch yourself saying, "the problem is ..." your problem is putting a dark lens over your vision.

Now that you've got a handle on how to convert a word to its energetic form, it's time to go a bit more in depth with the numerical meaning. To keep it simple, we converted "live," "problem," and "hate" to their final single-digit form, but there is more to the "energetic stew" of a word. The sum we arrived at before reducing to a single-digit number gives us an even more intimate view of what we're truly manifesting when we think, speak, or write a word.

"Live" adds to 21 before reducing to 3 and is written as 21/3. The 2 and the 1 add more energetic flavor to the word. The positive 2 is peaceful, supportive, and cooperative; the negative 2 is codependent and dualistic. The positive 1 is a leader or pioneer and is success-driven, but the negative 1 is egotistical, oppressive, and isolated. How we use "live" determines which sides of the 2 and 1 are most prominent (the positive or negative traits). When you add the 2 and 1 energies to the base energy of 3, the plot thickens, because the 2 and 1 are quite opposite energies, each with their own strong dualistic energies within them. So what does it mean to "live" from an energetic standpoint? You can be the inspirational (3), cooperative and supportive (2) leader or pioneer (1); or you can be the self-doubting (3), codependent and egotistical (1) loner.

Each word can have up to three energetic flavors, as we saw with the first three examples. "Live" has the energies of the 2, 1, and 3 (21/3); "problem" has the 3, 6, and 9 (36/9); and "hate" has the 1, 6, and 7 (16/7). When analyzing a word, optimally you'll want to note the meanings of all the numbers in the sum; for now, until you master the steps, the final single-digit sum will give you a good understanding of what you're manifesting.

CONTRACTIONS

A contraction is a shortened version of the written and spoken forms of a word, syllable, or word group, created by omission of internal letters. Some examples of contractions are "shouldn't," "couldn't," "can't," "won't," and "don't." Even though these contractions are comprised of two different words, the energy of the words merged creates a new energy and a separate word vibration. The combined contraction "couldn't" holds a different energetic vibration than the separate words "could not." If you normally use "couldn't" rather than "could not," the combined contraction is the word you need to explore further.

NAMES

Many cultures place a high importance on the name chosen at birth. For example, many Native American cultures and Chinese culture take names very seriously, but for different reasons. Names are very important in Chinese culture and are chosen carefully to ensure they bestow luck and wealth. In Native American cultures, names are usually chosen by the elders of the tribe and come to them in many different forms such as characteristics of the person being named, dreams that the elder may have, or the name of a family member who has died. In some tribes, it is deemed that two people in the same tribe cannot share the same name. Once the person with that name has died, then the name can be used again.

Your first name, last name, and birth names are important words in your life that should not be left out. Names are words, too, and because a name is a word used regularly, it affects your energy in a multitude of ways. Names in general, whether given to a person, place, or thing, are important on an energetic level and can affect the energetic tone you're sending out to the world.

Even if your birth name is not used every day, you carry its frequency with you from your birth. In numerology, names are thought of as your "mask," or how the world sees you through the expression of your personality. Although your full birth name (first, middle, and last given name) is rarely used except on things like legal or official documents and financial interactions, it carries an underlying vibration that represents your truest personality expression. Think of it as an energetic stamp you're given at birth. When you meet someone, your name vibration is one of the first energetic interactions they will have with you. What is it saying to them about you?

Your professional name is an energy used in your career or work life. People you interact with in a professional sense think of you through the vibrational frequency of your first and last name together. Depending on the career field, a stronger or softer name may be better or worse. Writers will often abbreviate their names with initials in combination with their last name or use a pen name, often due to a gut feeling or because another writer has a similar name and they want to be unique. If you're struggling in your career and there is no obvious outer reason, look to the name energy you are putting out there. A tweak like adding or subtracting an initial may allow you to appear in a completely different light.

My own name change was a pivotal time for me. I married my husband ten and a half years ago when I was six months' pregnant with my daughter. I don't follow any particular religious belief system and I've never been big on conformity, so getting married wasn't something that was high on my agenda. At the time, I was one of those people who thought of a marriage license as a useless piece of paper or an unnecessary technicality.

It was just before I discovered the numbers and numerology, so I was unaware of the significance the name change would bring for me. There was no doubt about my relationship with my husband and whether or not we would be together; we decided to marry not for us but more for the sake of our unborn daughter. I struggled with the idea of taking on my husband's name because to me it meant losing my identity. In hindsight, it was perfectly timed and exactly the energetic shift I needed.

My maiden name is Beek, which, when converted to its numerical equivalent, is the base number 5. My married name, Arbeau, has a base energy of 3. From a professional standpoint and in terms of my life purpose, my maiden name didn't fit the role I was about to step into as a numerologist. My first name is a 4 frequency; when added to my maiden name, the result is a 9 (4 + 5 = 9).

My pre-numerologist self was indeed a 9, the number of ambition, idealism, responsibility, and big-dreamer energy. At the time, I was working in human resources in the corporate world at a major bank, climbing the corporate ladder and dreaming of a better life than the nine-to-five grind. At the office, a coworker had nicknamed me "tell it like it is Michelle" because I was always the one to cut through the office politics and call out the elephant in the room. After I had my daughter, I decided I wouldn't be returning to the corporate world and my name change had a big part in steering the helm toward this new direction I was headed.

My first name added together with my new married name was a 7 (4 + 3 = 7). The 7 is the number of truth or the truth-seeker, and it reflected exactly whom I was but had yet to fully embrace at the time. As I was at the office, I was the truth-seeker, the deep and philosophical one who wanted to get to the bottom of whatever was presented in front of me. This, from day one, has been what numerology is all about for me—revealing the underlying truth in all things. The very name change that I initially resisted was the catalyst to align with my calling.

Whether you're Debbie, Donald, Kim, Bill, or Sara, what does your name say about your personality expression? Your first name is the name spoken most often, and it has the most energetic clout of all name combinations. The more a word is spoken, the more energy it is transmitting into your world. Your first name's vibration is a strong representation of how others see you on a day-to-day basis. A strong name vibration, such as the wise, independent, and assertive 8, can help you stand out as a leader while a softer name with the supportive and cooperative 2 vibration will highlight that you are support-ive and harmonious. Your name will attract the energies it sends out.

Parents need not worry that they have chosen the wrong name for their child. It's very rare to find a person whose name vibration does not suit their energy. If you are a new parent or a parent-to-be, you can take a look at the names you've chosen and I'm sure you'll be pleasantly surprised that you've chosen well. More will be discussed on the topic of names and nick-names in chapter 9.

Now that you've got the basic knowledge of what it means to convert a word to its energetic form, you can access the deeper meaning of any word.

In chapter 4, we'll begin the process of rewriting your per-sonal jargon into the positive and choosing your Top Ten Posi-tive Power Words by using the Top Positive and Negative Words reference section at the back of the book to give you a firm grasp on the vibration of the words you speak and how they can significantly affect your potential in all areas of life. You can't rewrite your life and truly manifest your vision until you completely understand the tool (word vibrations) you're using to create it.

Below are the 1–9 base number meanings that will serve as your reference for the energetic meaning of the words you con-vert with the word conversion chart in this chapter. All things, including words, can be reduced to these 9 base energy pat-terns based on the theories of the "father of numbers" himself, Pythagoras.

BASE NUMBER MEANINGS 1–9

1: The Pioneer

One (1) is the first physical-plane number. It governs our communications skills and verbal self-expression through the ego. It is the only complete number, representing our divine expression through the physical. As the number most linked to ego, it is a driven and active energy, seeking achievement and success. It is also the number of new beginnings.

Positive Keywords: verbal self-expression, initiate, action, ambitious, determined, and pioneering.

Negative Keywords: aggressive, egocentric, over-driven, self-absorbed, overachieving, and single-focused.

2: Supportive Guide

Two (2) is the first soul-plane number. It represents our dualistic nature as spiritual beings in a physical body. The 2 represents our need to find balance between these two opposing sides of ourselves. The 2 is the number of intuition, sensitivity, and co-operation.

Positive Keywords: balance, cooperation, sensitive, intuitive, supportive, and harmonious.

Negative Keywords: contrast, codependent, uncertain, submissive, passive, and hypersensitive.

3: Intellectual Socialite

Three (3) is the first mind-plane number. As the imaginative yet rational and analytical number, it represents left-brain activity. The 3 is of imagination and memory and is linked to the numbers 1 and 2. The 3's expression is directly tied to the intuitive and sensitive energy of the 2 and the verbal expression of the 1. The 3 is symbolized by the triangle and the mind (3), body (1), soul (2) connection.

Positive Keywords: analytical, intelligent, humorous, social, sensitive, observant, unity, and inspirational.

Negative Keywords: critical, vain, grandeur, self-doubting, self-critical, overanalyzing, and indecisive.

4: Practical Doer

Four (4) is the middle physical-plane number. It represents stability, steady progress, practicality, and organization. It is the "anchor" of the physical plane and is represented by the solid and stable construction of the square with four equal sides. It is the most primitive of numbers.

Positive Keywords: endurance, progress, foundation, practical, balanced, organization, solid, stable, and loyal.

Negative Keywords: materialistic, impatient, addictive, instant gratification, and self-absorbed.

5: Expressive Artist

Five (5) is the middle soul-plane number and is also the central number. The 5 symbolizes the heart and emotions; as the center number, 5 links the energies of all the other numbers. It is the "heart and soul" of the base numbers. The 5 must have freedom to express itself as erratic, free-flowing change energy. The 5 energy lends us the ability to see the world through the eyes of the soul.

Positive Keywords: loving, sensitive, irregular, artistic, freedom-seeking, passionate, and flexible.

Negative Keywords: uncertain, power-hungry, dominating, bossy, withdrawn, and moody.

6: Creative Visionary

Six (6) is the middle mind-plane number. It links both 3 (left brain) and 9 (right brain). It is the number of extremes with strong positive and negative sides. The 6 has an enormous amount of creative potential as the number of creativity, but when not positively creating, it can slip into the opposite (and negative) side of creativity—destruction. In the negative, 6 is dominated by worry, anxiety, and other negative thought patterns. In the positive, 6 can act as the "balancer" of the mind plane with its responsible, nurturing, and peace-making qualities.

Positive Keywords: creative visionary, certainty, balanced, nurturing, peace-making, optimistic, and forward-thinking.

Negative Keywords: pessimistic, judgmental, critical, "worry-wart," people-pleasing, doubtful, and gossipy.

7: Truth-Seeker

Seven (7) is the last and most active physical-plane number. As the teaching and learning number, it is high "doing" energy. The 7 learns through personal experience (often through hindsight), preferring to leap first and think later. Sacrifice and loss tend to be the rule of thumb for the 7 energy, but such learning sets the stage for accumulating a tremendous amount of knowledge and wisdom in a short amount of time, making 7 the self-made wise sage.

Positive Keywords: wise, contemplative, achiever, truth-seeking, determined, and hands-on.

Negative Keywords: stubborn, overactive, distrustful, hesitant, skeptical, and a loner.

8: Wise and Independent Leader

Eight (8) is the last and most active soul-plane number. It represents wisdom and independence. The 8 is confident, assertive, naturally wise, and a leadership energy. At the same time, 8 is loving and tender, wanting to love and be loved. These conflicting aspects of the 8 energy create its main lesson: to learn to recognize that openly expressing love and appreciation will not subtract from independence, but add to it.

Positive Keywords: wise, confident, assertive, independent, manifesting, assured, and loving.

Negative Keywords: detached, selfish, greedy, dominating, bossy, and attention-seeking.

9: Idealistic Humanitarian

Nine (9) is the last and most active mind-plane number. Although the 9 represents the right brain, it also combines the attributes of the other two mind-plane numbers, 3 and 6. Ambition (3), responsibility (6), and idealism (9) make up the whole essence of the 9 energy. Despite the idealistic and driven nature of the 9, it is a seeker of peace and justice and is considered the humanitarian number.

Positive Keywords: humanitarian, ambitious, responsible, justice-seeking, idealistic, and unselfish.

Negative Keywords: driven, opinionated, judgmental, critical, black and white, and narrow-minded.

CHAPTER 4

Your Top Ten
Positive Power Words

We all have a handful of favorite words we use often—maybe a little too often. The ten words you most frequently use on a regular basis could be the very reason you're not living the life of your dreams. The words and phrases we use on a daily basis carry the most energetic weight when it comes to their manifestation power because they're spoken so frequently. Words can uplift, inspire, and empower; they can also undermine, discourage, and block you from having what you desire. What are your words doing for you?

Choose Your Words Wisely

"Choose your words wisely" is more than a meaningless phrase your mother once used to remind you to speak positively. It's the next step in the art of successfully shaping your reality to match what you desire.

Social movements, such as cults, slavery, the Holocaust, Prohibition, and, more positively, the Green movement, have all been created by collective beliefs shaped by the power of words. Millions of people died during the Holocaust because of one man's view, and he used words to convince an army of men to do his bidding.

American slavery of the black culture was brought about by the views of a few perpetuated with words over generations. Although slavery pre-dates written records and has existed in many cultures, one of the slavery events most pertinent to today's world is that of the institution of American slavery. An estimated 12 million Africans arrived in the Americas from the sixteenth through the nineteenth centuries.[15] Of these, an estimated 645,000 were brought to what is now the United States. The views expressed or communicated by the elite society in the Americas were responsible for horrible acts of enslavement being accepted as commonplace. Even though today slavery is outlawed in most places in the world, it still exists prevalently, likely due to continuing collective consciousness beliefs set in motion many centuries ago. This is truly evidence of the power of words to shape the world.

The Green movement has been initiated through scientific studies. Many corporations use "Green-focused" words as marketing tools to leverage this movement that has caught on like wildfire. For example, the reduce-reuse-recycle logo, which was designed for a contest held on the original Earth Day in 1970, has since become a widely known symbol.[16]

Given the above examples, it would seem that words can be mesmerizing, hypnotizing, and magical. How could one person or even a few shape the views of many by expressing their opinions and beliefs through words?

Energy is contagious. Think of the last time you were an innocent bystander in an argument. How did you feel after being present while hate-filled words whipped around the room? You probably didn't leave feeling fantastic, and you likely left the scene feeling nearly as attacked as the actual victims of the argument. This is how mass belief or collective energy is formed. Words are energy, and they transmit a frequency to any situation. They shape destinies, change minds, and sway even the most ingrained opinions and beliefs in an instant. This is the power of words.

CREATING YOUR LIST

Pay special attention to the words you think, say, and write for a full twenty-four hours. When you use a word you are aware of using frequently, jot it down on a piece of paper. At the end of the day, you will hopefully have the ten words you use the most (be honest with yourself). Perhaps check with your close family or friends to see if they think it is accurate, but remember that many of the words will be words used in thought rather than speech. This list will change over time and you'll have to revisit and revamp it often to match what you want to create.

In going through this exercise, examine every area of your life to collect the most common words you use on a daily basis. We all wear different hats, depending on different situations that call for a range of vocabulary. Social situations, work life, and even your inner vocabulary will differ. Don't worry if you have more than ten to start—you can examine and put them in an order later. The more precise your list, the more precise your positive manifesting power can become.

Now that you've got your list, how does it look? A mostly positive list may only need to be tweaked, while a nasty negative list may need to be totally overhauled. If you've got the latter situation, it's not as dire as it seems. In fact, the solution is at your fingertips—pick up your pen and rewrite your life!

Your list might look something like this:

believe

awesome

can't

hope

no way

won't

love

best

whatever

problem

maybe

Using the steps outlined in chapter 3: "Determining the Vibration of a Word through the Language of Numbers" along with the alphanumeric word conversion chart, convert your ten words to their vibrational forms. Beside each word, write the energetic definition based on the number meanings in chapter 3.

The list in front of you is your new energetic exercise program. It will take a bit of time to change your ways and give your negative words the boot for good. Practice makes perfect, and time is on your side. Place sticky notes around the house, change your computer passwords to match your new words list, or pick a new "word of the day" to use as much as you can. These are all ways you can retrain your brain to integrate a more positive word list. The simple fact is, when you surround yourself with positive people, places, or things, your energy shifts into the positive, too. Regardless of your current circumstances, changing your words from negative to positive is something you have total control over in this moment. It won't be long before you'll see your hard work paying off in big ways. In chapter 5, there will be more specific ideas and tricks for integrating a more positive word list.

Using examples from your Top Ten Positive Power Words, let's examine how you might use those words in the context of a sentence. A word can have a different energetic meaning depending on how you use it. Keep in mind that the ingrained dictionary definition of a word will have an impact on how you feel about it, adding to its energetic impact.

First, let's examine the word "believe"; by the dictionary description, it means "to have confidence or faith in the truth." Used in the positive, this word can inject some real manifesting juice. "I believe I can achieve my goal" or "I believe in you" are very powerfully positive phrases. However, an alternative dictionary meaning paints a different picture. A less-upbeat definition is "to suppose or assume." When you say, "I believe he was going to get that done," the underlying tone is one of uncertainty instead of trust. If you use "believe" in the latter context, you're certain to create uncertainty in your life.

Numerically, "believe" is a 33/6 vibration. In the positive, 6 sprinkles creativity and the double 3 infuses inspiration and imagination. In the negative, the 6 brings worry and pessimism and the double 3 doles out self-doubt and criticism. So in considering the meaning, think about how you use the words most often.

Next are the words "no way." Although this is a phrase rather than a single power word, two-word phrases have a right to be on your list if you use them frequently. In this case, "no way" is used more like one word than two.

"No way" has a 24/6 vibration. With this word, although we can say it in a more optimistic tone when we hear something incredible or unbelievable ("no way!"), this word does not have a strong positive side. When you speak the phrase, you are literally saying there is no way (no solution, no path, etc.). The codependent, whiny 2 joins forces with the impatient and impractical 4 to form the worrywart, pessimistic 6. Using the phrase "no way" closes doors and shuts down opportunities that might be manifesting in the ethers.

"Whatever" is a wishy-washy word that seems to be most popular and used most often by the younger generations. A typical scenario would be a parent saying, "Do your chores" and the teen replying in a nonchalant tone, "Whatever." The underlying energetic vibration of "whatever" clearly matches the casual and vague way in which it is most often used, as it reflects the bright, sunny, social-butterfly energy of the 3. The

3 is inspirational, imaginative, and optimistic, but also quite indecisive in the negative, suffering from self-doubt and self-criticism. There isn't much drive or determination behind it and it is lacking clear direction. It's best to avoid words like "whatever" that don't allow you to move purposely ahead in the direction of your desires.

The word "can't" is a very common word that we're all guilty of using, but it is one of the most dream-squashing words of all time. You can use it in what seems like a positive way such as "I can't be held back" but there are much better words to choose. This word is the epitome of whiny as the 11/2 vibration. The double 1 adds a double-whammy egotistical essence, combining to create the codependent and uncooperative 2. Ego is all about fear and loves to view the glass as half empty.

Notice that, of the four examples we went through, only one was positive. This was purposeful, as the typical personal jargon list is more negative than positive to start off with.

Going through some of these powerful word examples has probably got your mind churning about your own personal jargon list and where it needs some improvement. Don't expect to change your list overnight. It will take time to make the new words a habit, but once you do, expect your manifestation power to kick into high gear.

CHANGING THE LIST

Focusing on changing or implementing one word at time will make the changes happen more quickly and be more likely to stick.

Using the Top reference section at the back of the book with some of the most commonly used positive and negative words, begin rewriting your Top-Ten Positive Power Words. Look at each word on your list one at a time. If there is a more positive version of a word on your list, try to use it in place of the more negative word. Some words on your list may need to be crossed off altogether and replaced with a new favorite word.

The key to writing your revised list is to have it match not only what you precisely want to create but also to ensure you're not creating what you don't want. "Can't" and "problem" are two great examples from the "creating what you don't want" category. Switch out those mostly negative words for new positive ones and watch your life switch from the negative to the positive.

The example list above might look something like this when rewritten positively:

believe

awesome

know

trust

absolutely

powerful

love

best

always

allow

fearless

The words "problem," "whatever," "won't," "can't," "no way," "hope," and "maybe" were booted off the list and replaced by the more positive power words "trust," "always," "allow," "powerful," "know," "absolutely," and "fearless." Your final list after this exercise should reflect areas you are striving to improve or manifest in your life. For example, thinking, speaking, or writing the word "powerful" just makes you feel good and instantly centers you in your own creative power.

In the example, the entire list needed to be rewritten except for two words: "love" and "best." You may find that your complete list needs to be redrafted, or just a few words. Those who fall into the latter category might have less of a challenge ahead of them, but those in need of a total rewrite will likely experience the most radical transformation if they're willing to put in the effort.

You don't need to fuss over this list in an attempt to perfect it. It will change as your life changes. Go with your gut and write the words as they come. Using your intuition for this exercise will reveal any areas you need help with transforming first, and allow you to utilize your full creative potential. Also look to areas in need of improvement that you're already aware of. If you have trouble trusting, the word "trust" should be on your Top-Ten Positive Power Words list. If it's a challenge for you to pinpoint specific areas of your life in need of improvement or your intuition radar seems on the fritz, begin by choosing words based on how they make you feel.

Your list isn't meant to be the one and only list; it's more like a pocket guide or quick reference to get you started. Keep a copy of the list on your car visor. Put it on sticky notes on your bathroom mirror or your workplace computer—anywhere you'll notice it often. Once you've got that list down, write another one and repeat. You can never have too many positive words in your vocabulary.

In chapter 6: "Personalized Affirmations that Really Work," we'll go more in depth with exploring ways to firmly establish tendencies with your new positive words list. You don't necessarily want to refer to your use of vocabulary as habit because the words you use should have conscious thought behind them and not be automatic responses. However, we are creatures of habit, and it works well to practice implementing new word lists to become more familiar with them.

The great thing about positive energy is that it's contagious. Once you've shifted your personal jargon list into the positive, those around you will soon be feeling your good vibes, too. Think of someone you know who seems to radiate positivity: how do you feel around them? Chances are this person is using positive words, too. Surrounding yourself with positive people, places, and things is one of the most important rules of manifesting what you desire. Small changes to the words you use can result in big changes in how and what you're creating in your life.

Setting yourself a goal of thirty days to incorporate your Top words into your daily vocabulary is a perfect way to help you keep your eye on the prize. Choose two or three words a week and focus on them—eat, sleep, and breathe your words!

Practice Makes Perfect

As creatures of habit, it can be tough to change what is ingrained. Old habits die hard, and it can take a lot of elbow grease to change our personal vocabulary list. Thankfully, habits are patterns, and with effort, patterns can be replaced with new ones. One of the reasons we're a habit-forming species is that our brain is wired to recognize and make sense of patterns, so you'll need to retrain your brain to recognize a new vocabulary pattern.

This chapter will take you into the "meat and potatoes" of how to change the stubborn vocabulary that may be hindering your success through the use of seven tried-and-true habit-busting practices. You've learned a lot about language and words so far, and now it's time to put that knowledge into action. As spiritual beings in a physical body, we may not be perfect, but in the case of changing the words we use, practice makes *improvement*.

Rule 1: Positive equals Positive

When wanting to become more positive in any way or form, surround yourself with positive people, places, and things. There are many people who subconsciously act as magnets for drama, gravitating toward people who have an exciting and action-packed life but with a focus on the negative. Are you one of these drama magnets? It's time to check yourself for the presence of this nasty habit by taking inventory of your friend list, your hangout joints, and even the food you consume. How do negative people, places, or foods make you feel? Are they predominately positive or negative? Start weeding out the negative stuff to shift gears into the positive.

Consider negative media, junk food, and drama queens to be just a few of the things on your off-limits list. You need to provide the right medium to grow a new vocabulary list.

In situations where you aren't able to completely remove yourself from the presence of the negative, choose to tune it out or shift your focus to the positive things around the scenario. Ricky Powell, a celebrity client of mine who is still building his brand as the Happiness Guy (apart from his day job as a director at NBC), says he chooses not to allow the negativity of working in the media and entertainment industry to affect him by shifting his attention toward only the positive things around him. This didn't happen in one day for Ricky; it took a great deal of effort, determination, and tricks, such as personalized positive affirmations (more in chapter 6 on this), to keep him focused in the positive.

Rule 2: Write It Down!

Sticky notes are a handy little tool for remembering things we might forget. Rarely would you come across someone who hasn't used these little paper gems at some point. So grab your stack of sticky notes and start writing! This is an old trick many books have cited as a means to remembering positive affirmations. Because it has been proven to work, it's worth implementing with your own personalized affirmations, too. Start by writing down your Top Ten Positive Power Words and simply stick them where you'll regularly see them. Make multiple copies if you need to put them in other places you spend a lot of time in, like the office or car.

Rule 3: Hit Repeat

When children are learning words for the first time, they tend to repeat the same word over and over until they master it. Think *Sesame Street* and pick a word of the day or week and focus on it. Use that word over and over again, as much as you can, until you feel confident you've integrated it into your permanent vernacular. Try incorporating it into your sentences, whether you're speaking or writing. It's much easier to bite off a small chunk of your vocabulary list and work on it bit by bit. Approaching it in this way ensures you're more likely to succeed because you won't feel overwhelmed or discouraged by not seeing any initial progress.

Rule 4: Broaden Your Horizons

One of the reasons we get stuck using negative vocabulary is the negative outlook or perception we often hold. "I can't do it" or "what if …" are phrases we use when we're being more narrow-minded in our thinking. Leave the door open wider for the possibilities and you'll find that you will automatically tend to use more positive phrases like "I can do this." Practice being the optimist who sees the glass as half full. Catch yourself in the act of trying to envision the negative outcome of a situation or judging yourself before you've even done something. Broaden your horizons. Not only does it give you permission to feel more positive, it also serves as an instant facelift for your vocabulary, too. It's much less likely that a negative word will slip from your lips when you feel optimistic.

RULE 5: BUDDY UP

Sometimes we need a little support when it comes to breaking habits. Change is challenging, and if you don't have to do it alone, don't. AA is a prime example of a very successful pattern-busting support system. Partnering with a buddy who is also trying to shift into the positive will help to keep you more focused and on track. After all, two heads are better than one! Be sure that your partner is serious about changing and that he or she is on your "positive people" list. As buddies, you can help each other through the times when you temporarily lose sight of your goals, question your success, or just have a bad day when you slip a bit. Set goals together and leverage each other to stick with them. You will greatly increase your chances of success this way. Ask someone you know who has lost a lot of weight or quit smoking about how they managed to stick with it. Most, if not all, will tell you they didn't do it alone but had a great deal of support from others. At the same time, they couldn't do it FOR anyone else—they had to make the choice that they really wanted it for themselves before it could be a lasting change. If you've got a mildly negative vocabulary list needing only a few minor tweaks, then you may be able to do it alone. But if your list is particularly nasty, complete with daily use of profanities, you definitely can't afford to skip this step.

Rule 6: Climb the Charts

Break out the washable markers or box of crayons, make a chart, and give yourself some gold stars for your achievements along the way. Remember how great you felt when your teacher gave you a star on your spelling assignments? Visually seeing your achievements on a chart will go a long way toward keeping you focused on your path. We all like a good pat on the back for a job well done, so give yourself one. Stick your chart on the fridge or your cubicle at work and look at it often. Cross off the words you've mastered as you go, and if you're feeling confident with conquering your current list, add new ones, too. Charting helps us to feel in control and on track, especially those of us who might be classified as "control freaks." If you're not into charting, at least aim to reward yourself regularly in other ways like buying yourself something special or treating yourself to your favorite restaurant dish. Just be careful not to overindulge in that celebratory chocolate mousse or have too many champagne toasts to your success or you'll have more habits to break than when you started!

Rule 7: Become a Wise Sage

This may be your first strategy to implement, because if you're not sure where to start in your search for positive life-altering replacement words, your first step is to become informed. Inspirational books are a dime a dozen, and it's a matter of personal preference. Go to your local bookstore or library and visit the self-help section in search of positive and inspirational books. Choose the books that call to you. Set aside time each day to delve into them, making note of words and phrases that strike a chord with you or make you feel good. The Internet is also a great smorgasbord of positive words, phrases, and inspiration if you look in the right places.

There is a twofold benefit to be gained from filling your head with positive information. Not only do you get to round out your new positive vocabulary list more easily than having to think them up on your own, you also get the added benefit of another source of daily positivity to keep you going strong.

You can even take this strategy a step further and *become* the wise sage. Start by shaking things up in your life and rearranging your other patterns. You don't have to quit your day job and go meditate on the top of a mountain, but do aim to reorganize how you approach the day. Some of the great spiritual leaders do things differently than the rest of us. They may still have busy schedules and lots to do, but they approach things with more awareness instead of going through life on autopilot. Be more mindful of the other things you're doing in life and you'll automatically begin to be more mindful of the words you're choosing to use. Do you start your day by stumbling out of bed and putting the coffee pot on? Why not take a refreshing shower first? You might just find you'll pass on that morning caffeine fix. Take the scenic route home through the countryside instead of getting stuck in the daily traffic jam. Consider rearranging your house or clearing out the clutter to better suit the more positive you. The ideas are limitless and you can customize them to fit your life—have fun with it! Breaking or changing old patterns makes way for new ones to form.

You now have seven effective ways to help you practice permanently and easily shifting your vocabulary from negative to positive. This list isn't comprised of the "be-all, end-all" strategies to switch your vocabulary into the positive, but it will certainly get you started and get your mind churning with your own strategies. One of the best perks of going through the seven habit-busting strategies in this chapter is that you'll find many areas of your life showing improvement—maybe some you didn't expect. Imagine going to work as Positive Patty instead of Negative Nelly—it would create a chain effect in the office! By broadening your perspective, filling your world with positive things, and finding a pep "buddy" to share the journey with, you're sure to begin shifting not only your vocabulary but your whole life. Positivity is contagious and will soon permeate your inner and outer life on all levels.

Remember, the goal isn't simply to cut out profanities or become the latest spiritual guru with all your inspirational words; the underlying reason for shifting your vocabulary is to shift your life into the positive to manifest your desires. Keep your eye on the prize while following the steps in this chapter and you'll reap the rewards you seek.

Personalized Affirmations That Really Work

Chances are, you've got a positive affirmations book some-where on your bookshelf collecting dust. If you're like me, it's likely not one of your all-time favorites and you probably don't even remember the name of it.

Most affirmation books are general, and as a result, not as helpful as they could be. They have an abundance of cheery words and inspirational phrases, but when you attempt to apply them in your own life, they feel somewhat like soda that lost its fizz. To invoke real and lasting change using positive af-firmations, you need to truly feel an affirmation with every fiber of your being.

Think of a time when you read an inspirational quote just when you needed it and it deeply resonated with you. The key to being successful with using affirmations is to not only understand the process intellectually but to connect with it emotionally and spiritually as well. If an affirmation doesn't resonate with you, toss it. It will be only a bunch of pretty words that are rather meaningless to you and may even do more harm than good. Let's say you're trying to lose weight and you use the affirmation "I am thin." While it is a positive statement, it's likely not going to help you feel or stay motivated to lose weight—quite the opposite! You'll likely end up feeling more self-conscious that you're not thin *yet*.

How do we create our own personalized positive affirmations that we'll stick with? Here's the part where you've got to dig deep within yourself and pull out those remaining negative records playing (over and over) to rewrite them into some fresh new jams.

Start off by examining the negative words on your personal jargon list. Why do you think you use those words and in what situations do you find yourself using them? Do certain people or places trigger you to use them? Most often we use negative words when we're fearful, insecure, or feeling low, but some are so ingrained that we tend to use them all the time, making it harder to nail down the reasons why we use them. Some words can be cleaned from your list simply by choosing to associate with more positive people, while other words we use as a crutch or armor to shield us from being hurt and aren't as easily interchangeable.

STEP 1: IDENTIFY YOUR NEGATIVE PATTERNS

This is easier than it sounds, and you don't need to make an appointment with your therapist to uncover these. For many of us, the majority of the negative patterns or "broken records" in our minds were created during our childhood and adolescence. Look back to your youth for traumatic experiences that stand out. Chances are, these bad memories were the start of one of the negative patterns hindering your life now. Were you bullied in school? Did you live in an abusive household? Were you extra skinny or overweight as a child? Always got C's when your friends got A's and B's? Also, look to your adult life: Did you go through a divorce? Are you repeatedly unlucky in love? Do you seem to attract poverty, creating financial stress? Does your boss belittle you or your work performance? Some of the old patterns from childhood may have been reshaped further by additional experiences as an adult. Talking with someone close to you can be very helpful in assisting you with revealing these patterns.

The second part to this step is to identify how these experiences made you feel. This will help you to align the experience with the negative words on your jargon list (Step 2). Beside each experience, write a few words that come to mind about how the experience made you feel. Did you feel insecure, hurt, insignificant, angry, jaded, vengeful, sad, afraid, or threatened? Try to be as precise with your feelings as possible to narrow in on your truest perception of the experience.

Step 2: Choose the Right Words
to Change Your Pattern

Once you've got your list of not-so-pleasant experiences and words representing how they made you feel, compare those experiences (and words) to your negative jargon list and pair up a word on the list with the experience you believe caused you to start using that word.

If you discover after reviewing your negative jargon list that you tend to say "I can't" because, as a child, you were told by an adult that you'd never amount to anything, using the affirmation "I can" really isn't going to cut it. In this case, since there may be some deep-seated insecurity, you need to start broader and work your way in or you'll never buy what you're selling through the affirmations.

Referring back to the word conversion chart in chapter 3 and the word-meaning reference section at the back of the book, examine some of the more positive words to swap out for the word "can't." A perfect substitute in this case would be the phrase "I am open," which allows for change but doesn't pressure you. Later on, you can move to "I can" when your pattern has shifted enough that you feel it resonates with you. The word "open" vibrates to the frequency of 5, which represents freedom of expression. You've now given yourself the freedom (but not the matter-of-fact pressure of "I can") to express yourself in any way you wish—large or small.

The name of the game is to utilize words as a tool to manifest the life we desire. The trick with creating your own unique affirmations is to match them to the negative patterns you want to change within you. While this is the basic goal of most affirmation books, you need to precisely pinpoint your *perception* of the pattern. Two people may share the same negative word in their daily vernacular list, but may have experienced completely different events that caused them to use that word. This is where the personalized tweaking comes in to shift your view of the experience or trauma that entrenched the pattern. Thus, you begin to attract what you do want and stop attracting what you don't want.

Some of the new words you'll be adding will come to you as a hunch while others may need to be carefully selected for their energetic meaning or flavor they infuse into the new pattern. Write down the words that stand out for you or that you're intuitively drawn to, narrow the list down, and concentrate on the words' energetic meanings.

Choosing the right positive words that match your individual needs and wants is essential to shift your negative patterns into the positive. Everyone's paths and experiences are different and require different frequencies of words to tip the scales into the positive. This is precisely why customized affirmations are so vital. So let's toss the outdated affirmations book like a fad diet and get back to the drawing board.

Suzy, a client of mine, uses several positive affirmations comprised of words she feels are right for her and has great success with them in terms of creating a sense of peace and harmony, which in turn assists her in attracting more positive vibrations into her life through the law of attraction. Previously, Suzy always felt she was "pushing uphill" and everything seemed difficult to accomplish with lots of obstacles constantly showing up in her life. After using mainstream affirmations from various books, which never truly resonated with her or brought her much success, she applied her own personalized positive affirmations. She was then able to focus on releasing control over the outcome of any situation, allowing it to manifest in the form it was meant to. Most importantly, it helped her relinquish her sense of a constant fear of failure. Now she believes she doesn't have to push so hard all the time. If it's meant to be, it will be:

> Sometimes when things feel especially trying and I need to stop pushing and just let things unfold as they will, I like to use "everything is unfolding in perfect divine order." This helps me to step back and give something time for the event to unfold as it was meant to. It's difficult to see why something is not happening at the time and in the way we think it should, but this affirmation reminds me that everything has a time and a place. It gives me inner peace and reassurance.

One of the key words in this positive affirmation is the word "perfect," which vibrates at the frequency of the perfect 10. It literally combines the energies of heaven and earth with the first physical number 1 and the 0, which is the symbol of the infinite or spiritual awareness. The word carries a balanced energy—body (1) and soul (0)—attracting additional people, places, things, and circumstances that are also resonating at this frequency.

STEP 3: HOW DO YOU WANT
TO REWRITE YOUR STORY?

Once you've matched up your negative words with the experiences that caused them, the last step in creating your customized affirmations is to change out the negative words for words with positive frequencies. Like the example above, substituting the words "I can't" with "I am open" pinpoints the energies that will allow you to move forward. If you sense you'll need to take baby steps at first with a particular pattern, choose a word with a frequency that gives you room to change and grow slowly but isn't pushing you off the cliff. Like all major changes, it's best to start slowly and work up to bigger steps. It will make the difference between success and failure, much like crash dieting versus simply eating healthier.

Here's an example of a common pattern to help you get started. When reviewing her childhood, Sara found that her most stand-out, memorably traumatic experience was from elementary school. Fourth grade was harsh for Sara. She was picked on because she was very skinny, shy, and got braces that year. One girl in particular bullied her at least a couple times a week, calling her "metal mouth," "beanpole," and "dumb blonde." The feelings she associated with that experience were insignificant, helpless, lost, and frustrated.

Sara's main issue in her current life is that she feels helpless much of the time, having to rely on others to help her make decisions, giving away her personal power, and being a doormat more often than not. Although Sara has a university degree with honors and is a successful lawyer, she admits she feels inadequate much of the time, especially in her personal life. Some of the words on her negative word list that she matched to this experience are: "well," "maybe," "if," and "whatever."

Armed with the knowledge she was giving away her personal power in her adult life because she felt helpless in the bullying situation as a child highlighted for Sara that she needed to regain a sense of personal power in her present life. Choosing powerful and self-assured words like "certain," "yes," "absolutely," and "capable" to replace her negative words has allowed Sara to regain her sense of personal power. From an energetic standpoint, the new energies she infused into her life were self-trust ("certain" = 7), solid foundation, ("yes" and "capable" = 4), and creative power ("absolutely" = 6). (Visit chapter 3 for complete number meanings.)

As you can see from Sara's example, it's that easy to reword your story in the positive. How long have you been living a mediocre life when you could have been living your best life? Don't wait another second—get out your pen and paper and reword your story to change your life!

Maximize Your Manifesting Power

If you're reading this book, there's a good chance you already know something about the law of attraction. For those of you less familiar, this chapter will give you the nuts and bolts of how to create the life you desire through the law of attraction combined with your newly learned missing key: the energy of words.

The spiritual laws that govern us on an unseen level are very much tied into the laws of physics—actually, they're one and the same. The basis of the law of attraction is very simple: like attracts like. We attract into our lives whatever we focus on. Here's a catchy phrase to help you remember this important law: what we think about, we bring about.

Unlike traditional science, which is based on a system that states everything is fixed with a predictable outcome or reaction based on an action applied, quantum physics is based on the theory that nothing is fixed and there are no limitations or constraints because the essence of all things is energy.

Quantum physics has often been referred to as the "science of possibilities," but the law of attraction takes it one step further by giving us direct control over our destiny. We are not at the mercy of our outer world but only bound by what we believe to be true. The thoughts we hold are the driving force behind the world we live in each day. The law of attraction works every time it is correctly applied, yet so many people aren't successful in using it and wonder why. Armed with the knowledge that thoughts shape our reality minute by minute and that any form of language is shaped first in the mind, it is clear that the words we choose to use are the key to successfully applying the law of attraction.

Recognize Doubt-Filled Words

There is no gray area with the law of attraction. This is precisely where most of us get caught up and why it doesn't always work consistently. Perhaps you've created a vision board, complete with a picture of your dream car, house, career, and partner. You look at it every day, putting a great deal of thought, focus, and feeling into imagining yourself having all of these things, but months go by and not a sign of any of them materializes. Most law of attraction books say this is where doubt starts to creep in, destroying any efforts or progress you might have made thus far. You start to doubt whether you will have that perfect car, house, or partner. Doubt is the number-one wrench that gets thrown into the machine of manifestation. Could it be that you were doubtful right from the start because you subconsciously infuse doubt-filled words into your daily life?

These doubt-filled words may not even be directly associated with what you've been attempting to manifest, but they would certainly hit the kill switch on your manifesting power.

Here's a prime example of why the law of attraction doesn't always work, even if you have the best of intentions, due to the words you choose to use on a daily basis. Mary was a Realtor who had worked very hard to climb to the top of the sales force. She had won many accolades and awards for being top seller and she was very pleased with her career. Her love life, however, was anything but successful. She was lonely, and because she was thirty, she felt her biological clock ticking. Her friends tried to set her up on dates, and though she met some really great men in the process, none of them felt "just right." Mary was a firm believer in the law of attraction because she had used it successfully many times in her career life.

Mary created a checklist of the qualities she desired in a potential partner and father to her children. She looked at this list every day before going to work, putting a great deal of thought and emotion into imagining her ideal mate.

Mary had no idea that the words she chose to use daily, which really didn't directly have anything to do with attracting her soul mate, were the very things that were hindering her from attracting the love of her life.

Mary was quite an indecisive person, especially in her social life, using phrases like "well, I don't know" and "maybe I will." Her energy was teeming with indecisive and wishy-washy energy, which translated into a lack of success with the law of attraction in her personal life. It wasn't necessarily that she doubted what she wanted in a partner—she was clear in that. It was the energy she was injecting into her life from the words she chose.

Mary was imagining the perfect man, but she counteracted her manifestation by using words that hold the frequency of doubt or indecisiveness. The energy she held created resistance in the form of doubt-filled words. The word "don't" vibrates to the frequency of 8; in the negative, 8 lacks its self-assured confidence, which is its main trait in the positive. "Maybe" vibrates to the 1; in the negative, 1 is very ego-focused as it is the only isolated number (not divisible by another number). We can't be clear in our decisions without consulting our soul for the truth; the result of not doing so is an unclear, on-the-fence thought process, which is the very definition of the word "maybe."

If you are consistently applying the law of attraction in your own life and not seeing your efforts manifesting your desires into physical reality, it's time to reexamine your daily personal word list and match it exactly to what you want to create. Everything is energy (including words), and that energy permeates every part of our reality.

Of all the things the law of attraction is used for, one of the most popular intentions is manifesting wealth in some form. There's a reason why only about 1 percent of the world's population holds all the wealth. The following example shows why.

Todd came from a very impoverished background during which his family struggled with money issues most of his childhood. He was proud that he had earned a university degree in business and was working in sales for a large marketing firm, given his financially challenged background growing up. He watched some of his friends who had the same childhood experiences go on to not amount to much, working menial jobs, continuing the financially challenged legacy passed on from their families. Todd vowed to himself that he wouldn't end up like that and worked hard to achieve his current level of success. Despite all his gains, Todd still found it difficult to feel comfortable with money. He felt he deserved to be paid more, yet part of him felt undeserving of it, even though he knew he was overqualified and underpaid for his current position. This was a common theme throughout his work life thus far: overqualified and underpaid.

Although he rarely showed his doubtful side at work, he admitted he often thought about the fact that he didn't truly feel deserving of more money. The word "deserve" vibrates to the energy of 6, which in the negative holds the qualities of pessimism, judgment, and criticism. Interestingly, in this case, Todd was using the correct word but in the wrong energetic context. The positive side of 6 is creativity, human effort, and self-nurturing. Simply by utilizing the power of the word "deserve" in the positive, Todd could create the financial abundance he'd been blocking for so long. An example of an affirmation Todd could use to attract financial abundance would look like this: "I deserve financial abundance because I've earned it."

It's clear that the law of attraction works, but if you feel it's not working for you, it's time to examine your approach from a broader viewpoint. It's a wonderful idea to have a checklist, vision board, or plan of action to assist you in manifesting what you want, but it is important to also comb through all areas of your life for opposing energies. For many, the key to those opposing energies is in the words you choose to use every day, regardless of whether or not those words seem to be directly related to what we desire.

CONSIDER YOUR FEELINGS

Let's not forget about the feeling factor with the law of attraction. It's not only in the words you choose to use, it's in the feelings you have about those words as well. In the example with Todd and his inability to attract strong financial abundance, he was using the right word but had the wrong feelings behind it due to his past experiences. His past experiences shaped his perception of the word "deserve." Feelings serve as amplifying "juice" to accelerate the manifestation process. Todd's underlying feelings of not being deserving of a higher salary played a huge part in his resistance of financial abundance. Shifting his feelings would have shifted the energy of the word "deserve" into the positive.

Taking control of your manifesting power boils down to identifying the negative patterns and the words you use that represent them. We all have our own unique life story that has been shaped by our personal experiences and perceptions of those experiences, but we can shift our view of the past at any time we choose.

Does your personal word list—whether thought, written, or spoken words—reflect more of your past experiences, present circumstances, or future desires? Your honest answer to this truth-revealing question will show you what you're manifesting in your life through the power of words.

A client who had a childhood full of poverty and verbal, physical, and sexual abuse came to see me because she was tired of struggling to succeed. Life seemed harder for her, and she complained that she had to fight for everything she had. Throughout our session, she repeatedly used the word "fight" to relay her challenges. The word "fight" vibrates to the base energy of the 5, the freedom of expression number. When 5 is in the negative, it can be power-seeking, dominating (Hitler's date of birth added to 5), and erratic. One of the things she prided herself on was that everything she did have, she had accumulated all on her own. She was a tough girl and had too much pride to ask for help in any way. I showed her that by using the word "fight" so frequently, she was literally creating more scenarios of struggle and hardship. I suggested she begin replacing the word "fight" with the word "work" whenever she could. "Work" is the frequency of the 22/4. As the master builder number (more on master numbers in chapter 10), it is a hard-working, stable, foundation number but also carries the supportive, cooperative, and harmonious double-2 energy. For my client, the word "work" replaced the erratic and dominating word "fight" and replaced it with an energy that said she was willing to put in the effort but wasn't opposed to receiving support and cooperation where appropriate, thereby attracting less isolated struggling. About six months after our session, through shifting her words and thus her viewpoint of her life, she manifested the opportunity to move to a different city with a better job. She could now support herself and her son without having to "fight" to achieve everything.

C H A P T E R   8

Words That Changed the World

Words have started and ended wars, built and destroyed nations, created peace, saved lives, launched life-changing movements, formed musical or literary masterpieces, and brought clarity or misunderstanding to people and situations for centuries. The power of words is unmatched in terms of human expression. No other form of communication has the ability to profoundly affect and drastically change both our inner and outer world like words.

Words can make or break a situation. Timing is everything, and it's another reason why we should choose our words wisely. We've all experienced saying the wrong thing at the wrong time or the right thing at the right time. Some words spoken we regret, while others we cherish as fond memories. Some words seem to stick with us even longer than the memory of the experience itself, and we are forever changed by them. Most often it is a result of a painful or traumatic experience. Think back to your first experience with a bully who embarrassed you with hurtful words; you can probably vaguely recall the experience visually, but you will most certainly and quickly be able to recall the mean words that were said to you. Most mothers can matter-of-factly tell you what their child's first word was, but may not be able to precisely describe the experience. Coma patients can often recall words spoken to them while unconscious. The effect of words on the psyche can be powerful and lasting; their energetic signature can leave a lasting mark on our psyche in both positive and negative ways.

There's no question that words are powerfully transformative and are responsible for many life-changing events on both personal and global levels. The vibration of a word is a highly personalized experience. Each person interprets and assimilates a word's energy differently, based on their unique energetic frequency and patterns. A word that cuts like a knife for one may roll off the back of another.

Those who are in a place of great power or influence have a greater responsibility to choose their words wisely. Instead of affecting just a few, they affect the masses and have the power to change the trajectory of the world with a single word. Kings, queens, world leaders, activists, inventors, scientists, CEOs, and celebrities have the ability to change a mass belief, sway common opinion, or start a worldwide trend using nothing but their words. Throughout history, world leaders and revolutionaries have shaped the world through words, and their linguistic legacy lives on today. Language is often taken for granted, its tremendous power going unrecognized. If you want to change your life and possibly the world, look to the words you are using every day because they are the missing link to manifesting all that you desire.

To get you started on the road to shaping your own life using the manifestation power of words, let's examine some of the words that have left a lasting mark on the world, and why they did. There are endless examples and only a handful are listed here, but this list will give you a window into the powerful force of words in the hands of those who truly recognize their power. Through reading these words of wisdom by great leaders, scientists, and pioneers, you will hopefully recognize you are also a powerful creator in your own life and your tool is the power of words.

Words That Launched a Movement
"Make love, not war."
This slogan was used in the 1960s by those opposing the Vietnam War. It caught on like wildfire and became the tagline for the hippie movement. The key words in this phrase that afford it such word power are "make," "love," and "war." "Make" vibrates to the 3, which is the number of unity; "love" is the humanitarian number 9; and "war" is 6, the number of creativity and human labor as well as pessimism, criticism, and judgment in the negative. It's plain to see why this slogan caught on so quickly and had a lasting effect during wartime. It is a very unifying (3), humanitarian (9), and creative visionary energy (6).

"I have a dream."—Martin Luther King, Jr.

This phrase was from a seventeen-minute public speech by Martin Luther King, Jr. delivered on August 28, 1963, in which he called for racial equality and an end to discrimination. The speech, from the steps of the Lincoln Memorial during the March on Washington for Jobs and Freedom, was a defining moment of the American civil rights movement.

The key words in this phrase pack a powerful punch of idealism, responsibility, inspiration, and optimism. "Have" is the 9 energy with its idealistic, ambitious, and responsible essence. "Dream," as the positive and sunny 3, is the number of unity, inspiration, and imagination; not only is it a 3, it actually adds to 12 first before reducing to 3 (1+2=3), and 12 is considered the whole and complete number in numerology. "Dream" joins the pioneering and driven 1 with the peaceful, cooperative, and harmonious 2 to create the number of unity—the 3. This phrase stands out in Dr. King's pivotal speech because, on an energetic level, it brings hope, inspiration, optimism, and a sense of unity as well as placing the creative manifesting power (3) back into the hands of the people.

"Knowledge is power."—Francis Bacon

This sentence is found in the works of Francis Bacon and has become a catchphrase associated with the belief that knowledge is fundamental in terms of our advancement and growth as a society. "Knowledge" has 6 energy, the creative visionary number; "power" has 5 energy, the heart-centered freedom of expression number. Together they energetically send the message that with knowledge, we have the creativity and visionary capability (6) as well as the freedom (5), and therefore, power, to achieve anything.

WORDS THAT CHANGED OUR PERCEPTION

"All religions, arts, and sciences are branches of the same tree."—Albert Einstein

"Branches" and "same" give this quote its lasting effect. "Branches" holds the energy of the 7, which represents the deep, philosophical, truth-seeker essence; "same" has the root vibration of 3, the number of unity. Not only does this quote translate literally into saying religion, art, and science come from the same source, it energetically translates that way as well.

"Time is money."—Benjamin Franklin

Time and money are two things that the civilized world has paired together for a long time, yet interestingly enough, from an energetic standpoint, they couldn't be more different. "Time" is a 2 vibration, the number of peace, harmony, and cooperation; "money" is a 9 vibration, the number of ambition, idealism, and responsibility. One represents more spiritual qualities (2) while the other more ego-dominated qualities (9). If we look at the previous century, the 9 ruled the show, creating a level of advancement and achievement in all areas of society that is unmatched in any other time period. Everyone had at least one 9 in their date of birth as well, giving each person born in the 1900s the drive, determination, and ambition of this active mind-plane number. When we turned the page into the twenty-first century, the ambitious 9 was replaced by the cooperative 2 energy, and sure enough, cooperation-based ideology, such as the Green movement, has swept in.

Benjamin Franklin was "right on the money" with his phrase "time is money"; our cooperative efforts (2) as a society allowed us to achieve great levels of success and achievement (9), including monetary accumulation. The downside to phrases like Franklin's is that they create a negative societal belief or thought pattern. In Franklin's quote, money is more precious than time, and we should sacrifice our time for monetary gain.

"That's one small step for a man, one giant leap for mankind."—Neil Armstrong

The world was captivated and in awe of the moon landing, but even after the visions of that event faded in our minds, the first words from the lips of the first man on the moon still live on vividly. The important words in this phrase are "man" and "mankind." These two words focus on "me" as a single entity and "we" as a whole. Broken down, "man" is a 1 vibration, the isolated and more ego-based energy; "mankind" is the 3 energy, the number of inspiration, imagination, and unity. We are a micro (1) of the macro (3), or a piece of the whole.

The common thread with all of these life-changing phrases is the shift in perception that they create. When you hear words that seem to stir something inside and a feeling of resonation washes over you, it is the energy of the words shifting an energetic pattern within you.

CHAPTER 9

Role-Playing with Words

Throughout history, many word labels have been given to various common roles or states of existence like mom/dad, teacher/student, king/queen, master/servant, god/goddess, parent/child, leader/follower, lover/fighter, winner/loser, man/woman, friend/enemy, daughter/son, heaven/earth, war/peace, good/evil, hero/villain, etc. These labels emerged at various times and for various reasons, but what do they really mean from an energetic standpoint?

Ever wonder why it's the social norm to call your parents Mom and Dad? Like the origin of language, which is still under debate, the origin of the titles we automatically assign to parental figures remains somewhat of a mystery as well. One of the most universally accepted roles is that of mom or dad. Depending on the language spoken, the pronunciation may be different, but the meaning is very similar throughout many cultures and races. Most of us associate our parental figures with unconditional love, support, and gentle leadership; in the energetic sense, that's just what these titles radiate.

MOM/DAD

The perfect image of a mom is that of love, tenderness, and nurturing. The word "mom" is the frequency of the 5, the number of the heart and emotions representing freedom of expression. The mom has traditionally been viewed as the one to care for the young.

The father figure in the family is often painted as the leader or head of the household in many cultures. He is usually the breadwinner, the "hunter," and the disciplinarian. The word "dad" vibrates to the number 9, the idealistic, ambitious, humanitarian energy. As we discussed in chapter 8, 9 is responsible for the vast amount of achievement and success during the 1900s, as everyone had at least one 9 in their date of birth. The 9 is a leadership energy, but less about preaching from the mountaintop and more about getting in the trenches with the people. Many movies, TV programs, and books have depicted "mom" and "dad" in this light for years, making it somewhat of a socially accepted vision of our parental figures.

There is an alternative side to these roles; not all parents fit the positive side of their roles as a loving and nurturing mom or a dad who is a gentle leader, humanitarian, and disciplinarian. The negative sides of the 5 and 9 portray a very different version of "mom" and "dad."

The 5 in the negative indicates "mom" is detached, moody, power-hungry, and freedom-seeking. The 9 in the negative indicates "dad" is critical, judgmental, opinionated, and narrow-minded. Depending on your personal experiences with your own parental figures, you might resonate with either the positive side or the negative side of these parental roles. Was "mom" the typical domestic goddess or was she a working mother who wasn't home as much as you wanted her to be? Was "dad" the gentle yet firm shoulder to lean on or the extra-strict and critical disciplinarian?

Regardless of your upbringing or your parents' influence, the labels of "mom" and "dad" have an energetic effect on the way you perceive those roles. Your experiences that included and continue to include those labels/roles play a part in molding and shaping your reality. The energetic frequency you hold for the label of "mom" or "dad" can be relayed to your relationship with your children, friends, or intimate partners. Do you view "mom" and "dad" in the positive or negative?

Labels Shape Our Present and Future

The words you use to label others or yourself also have a significant impact on how you view your own roles and the roles of others. Even using a nickname or getting married and taking on your spouse's last name energetically shifts your frequency and thus your role in life.

When parents name a child at birth, they are placing a title or label on the child for life, unless the individual chooses to change it. Our name shapes us in terms of how we express our personality and as a label is more an outer piece of our energy or external influence.

It's common to hear someone say, after getting a name wrong, "Sorry, you look like a Lisa." We associate certain traits and characteristics with common labels and there is more to it than just familiarity. The energy these labels hold are patterns we subtly recognize on an intuitive level. A label can set the tone of a relationship.

Let's briefly examine the remaining label examples listed at the beginning of the chapter to get a better idea of how labels affect how we view certain roles and individuals.

Teacher/Student

We all have memories of teacher/student relationships, probably both good and bad. How did these role labels impact our experiences during those formative years? "Teacher" vibrates to the 33/6 energy, which is actually the master teacher number. It combines the intelligent and inspirational double 3 with the creative expression and visionary number 6 to inspire (3) the student to see the bigger picture (6). The master numbers are written in their full forms before reducing to a single digit, as they hold a special frequency as a guiding energy.

"Student" is also a master number, the master builder, 22/4. The 22/4 combines the intuitive double 2 with the enduring, progressive, foundation-building 4 to make "student" a receptive and open (2) yet hard-working energy (4).

King/Queen

Many cultures throughout the centuries have had kings and queens, and the image most of us have of these labels or roles is that of dictator or ruler. In the negative, that image isn't far from the truth as these labels vibrate to the 5 and 8, the most dominating and power-hungry energies in the negative.

"King" is the 5, the number of the heart/emotions representing freedom of expression. In the negative, the 5 is power-hungry, moody, and detached. Hitler, although not a king per se, was a powerful dictator who fully lived through his main essence as the 5 (his date of birth adds to 5), but used the negative side of the 5.

"Queen" is the 8, the number of confidence, wisdom, and independence. In the negative, the 8 is bossy, dominating, greedy, selfish, attention-seeking, and detached. Do you imagine a queen to be a wise and independent leader or a selfish and dominating diva?

Master/Servant

"Master" vibrates to the master builder number 22/4. A master can be a gentle leader in the positive, pulling from the intuitive and sensitive influence of the double 2 combined with the enduring and progressive foundation of the 4. Yet in the negative, it can be an impatient, materialistic, and self-absorbed leader.

"Servant" holds the energy of the 9, the selfless humanitarian willing to go the extra mile for anyone as it seeks to be of service. The faithful servant is indeed the unselfish, idealistic, and ambitious 9.

God/Goddess

"God" is a profound energy, regardless of religious beliefs. It carries a particularly powerful frequency that explains the essence and purpose of the word precisely. "God" means different things to different people, but for the purpose of this example, we will approach the meaning of "god" as being the macro and we are all a micro or a piece of the macro (God).

Although it is always the base energy (numbers 1–9) that matters in terms of discovering the main energetic frequency of any word, person, or thing, in the case of the word "god," it is important to examine the frequency of the sum before reducing as well. "God" vibrates to the 17/8. The 8 is of wisdom and independence, but upon closer examination, the 17/8 paints the story of what "god" truly is. It combines the verbal self-expression of the 1 with the deep and philosophical truth-seeker 7 to form the 8, which is the number of wisdom. As a micro of the macro, we are here to use our ability to verbally self-express (1) the truths of the divine (7) for the purpose of sharing knowledge and wisdom (8) to facilitate our soul's evolution.

"Goddess" is the master number 10, also called the earth-guide energy. The 10 combines the energies of heaven and earth as 1 is the first physical-plane number and 0 is the symbol of the infinite or spiritual awareness. A goddess has long been thought of as the embodiment of the spiritual realm or the supernatural in physical form, especially in Greek mythology.

PARENT / CHILD

"Parent" vibrates to the 2, which is the number of intuition, sensitivity, harmony, support, and cooperation. A parent is meant to protect, provide, and guide a child as it grows, and the 2 energy matches this definition perfectly.

"Child" is the 9 frequency, which is the number of ambition, idealism, and responsibility, but is also big-dreamer energy. "Child" as the 9 energy is impractical and needs guidance to keep on track with idealistic big dreams.

The 2 and the 9 energies are completely opposite vibrations in many ways. The ambitious 9 is all about progress, determination, and achievement and the supportive 2 aims for peace, cooperation, and harmony.

LEADER/FOLLOWER

How many times have you heard the question, "Are you a leader or a follower?" "Leader" is the determined, ambitious, and idealistic humanitarian 9 energy, while "follower" is the seeker of truth number 7. "Leader" resonates with the black-and-white justice-seeking qualities of the 9, while "follower" seeks the answers without rather than within (7 lacks a sense of inner self-trust in the negative). So, are you a leader or a follower?

LOVER/FIGHTER

Are you a lover or a fighter? "Lover" embodies the selfless humanitarian 9 traits, driven only for others and putting themselves last. "Fighter" holds the essence of the trailblazing, pioneering, driven, new-beginnings number 1, the stand-alone, isolated number indivisible by any other number. It is a sole survivor, not needing anyone or anything to feel whole and complete.

WINNER/LOSER

"Winner" reflects the dualistic side of the 2 energy. In the negative, the 2 flips from peaceful, harmonious, supportive, and cooperative energy to expressing a more separated and dualistic frequency. "Winner takes all" is a common phrase and reflects the negative 2 energy at work. By this definition, to be the winner is to do it alone. From a positive viewpoint, "we're all winners" is the frequency of the supportive 2.

"Loser" is the pessimistic, whiny, doubtful, and judgmental 6 energy in the negative, as in the phrase "sore loser." In the positive, the creative visionary 6 sees beyond the current situation, assessing from a broader viewpoint; "loser," then, gains an optimistic tone that is much less bleak and self-defeating than the pessimistic worrywart 6. "You're not a loser, that game just isn't your thing."

MAN/WOMAN

In the caveman days, men were the hunters and women were the gatherers. "Man" is the pioneering, trailblazing, driven, and overachieving 1, which is the first physical-plane number. "Woman" is the inspirational, imaginative, and analytical 3, which is the first mind-plane number. Traditionally, the man has been seen as being physical-based while the woman has been considered the mental-based partner.

FRIEND/ENEMY

A friend is someone who is supportive, cooperative, harmonious, and sensitive; incidentally, that's exactly what the word "friend" means on an energetic level as the number 2. The 2 is a gentle, supportive energy. Behind every great leader, you'll typically find a 2; this is what we all want when it comes to a friend.

An enemy is quite the opposite of the gentle and supportive 2. "Enemy" vibrates to the 8, the assertive and independent number. In the negative, the 8 is detached, bossy, dominating, and selfish. If you've ever had an enemy, you know the negative qualities of the 8 fit the bill.

DAUGHTER / SON

This pair of labels is an intriguing combination, as both resonate with the inspirational, imaginative, and unifying 3 energy. As the number of unity, "daughter" and "son" both represent the coming together of a man and woman to create a child. With both being the same frequency, it confirms that neither one is better than the other and both are reflections of unity. When parents speak these labels to their children, the underlying tone or energetic message is a reminder of what they have created through their coming together.

HEAVEN / EARTH

"Heaven" and "earth" are two labels that are a bit different from the previous ones we've explored in this chapter because they don't represent people but rather places or things. Still, it is worth examining these kinds of labels, as it can show you what outlook you hold on them.

"Heaven" personifies the number 10, which literally carries both the physical (earth) and the spiritual (heaven). The first physical-plane number (1) joins forces with the symbol of the infinite or spiritual awareness (0) to create the frequency of the earth-guide number 10. Both the word "heaven" and the meaning of its energetic vibration of the 10 bring more validity to the belief that there is an intangible world of spirit beyond the physical. The phrase "heaven and earth collide" rings true here.

Earth is the most active physical-plane number 7, representing what we are here on earth to do: actively create in the physical through personal experience. The 7 is the teaching/learning number and the truth-seeker energy. The purpose of the 7 is to gather wisdom and knowledge to reveal the deeper truth through the acts of personal experience. It is a popular belief in the metaphysical community that we are here to attend this "earth school" as a means of gaining experiences for the purpose of our soul's development. The energetic meaning of the word "earth" aligns with this theory.

WAR/PEACE

"War" is the creative visionary number 6. In the negative, the 6 is critical, pessimistic, and judgmental. The negative 6 loses sight of the bigger picture or purpose and becomes narrow-minded and critical. "War" holds the essence of the negative 6.

"Peace" is all about unity as the inspirational, imaginative, and unifying 3. In fact, "peace" adds to 21 before reducing to 3 (2 + 1 = 3), representing the intuitive, sensitive, harmonious, and cooperative 2 joining together with the pioneering, trailblazing, achieving, and new-beginnings energy of the 1.

GOOD / EVIL

"Good" is the compassionate, loving, heart-centered, and freedom-seeking 5. In the positive, 5 seeks to make use of the loving energy it holds by being of service in some way. Those people, places, or things considered good are often thought of as pure of heart or a "feel-good" energy. "He's a good person through and through."

"Evil" is the intelligent, imaginative, and inspirational 3. The phrase "evil genius" is a perfect representation of what the label "evil" stands for. In the negative, the 3 is self-doubting, self-critical, critical of others, and acts mentally superior. Those people, places, or things classified as "evil" usually have a dark and negative side associated with them that is fraught with insecurities like self-doubt and criticism. "She's just pure evil and treats everyone horribly."

HERO / VILLAIN

Heroes are depicted in many movies, books, and stories as those who are called to action in a selfless way, coming to our rescue in a time of need. "Hero" adds to 10 before reducing to 1 (1 + 0 = 1) giving a sense of spiritual depth to the pioneering, trailblazing, and driven isolated 1 while 0 is the symbol of the infinite or spiritual awareness. A hero typically acts alone (1) but is selflessly acting for the purpose of helping someone, which is where the power of the 0 deepens the hero's call to action beyond just the physical pull of the number 1 as the first physical-plane number.

"Villain" vibrates to the distrustful, detached, hesitant, skeptical, and stubborn 7 in the negative. The villain is usually highlighted as the "bad guy" in the storyline. However, given the positive side of the 7, which is the trust-filled truth-seeker, it shows that the "bad guy" isn't pure evil and can have a good side, too.

NAMES AND NICKNAMES

Whether you like your name or not, it seems that being named is one of those haphazard events life over which we have no control; our parents choose names to suit us or to fulfill the promise of a namesake. Regardless of how we acquired our name, there is more to a name than its face value.

Names represent our personality and how the world sees us. The frequency of a name gives an immediate energetic first impression of who we are and what we have to offer the world. In my own practice, I have had clients who felt strongly at a certain point in their life to change their name or tweak it to a new variation. Most often, it was because they were going through a shift in their path and wanted to align their name with their life purpose. One woman changed her name from Leah to Lia, and the vibration suited precisely the transition in career that she was about to make. She didn't make the connection at first on a conscious level, but felt the strong desire to change her name. Once we sat down and examined her name further, it was clear that the change was necessary. The change made a huge difference in assisting her transition from one career to her heart's calling.

Many people use nicknames as a replacement for their own name or the names of others in their life, often created as a pet name or to simplify the name. William becomes "Bill" or

"Will" and Joseph becomes "Joe" or "Joey"; how does that change the frequency of the name and how it affects the overall energy or essence of the person labeled with it?

Words as names can hinder or help us on our path; it's important to not forget about these pivotal words in life. If you've always felt a strong desire to change your name but have resisted the urge until now, it might be time to reconsider. Here's a prime example from a client of mine in Beverly Hills, California, who felt like she had a new lease on life after changing her last name:

> Until last year, I never really thought much about a name or my name in particular. It was last October, just before I was about to speak live in front of an audience for the very first time. I was at dinner with my parents. I remember being so excited that I was going to speak because it was a big deal for me; I had always been "shy, until I got to know someone," and it was only a couple of months before that dinner I started to come out of my shell.
>
> Unfortunately, my parents didn't share that same excitement. As I was out to dinner with them, happily talking about how honored I felt to be asked to speak and how amazing it made me feel, the bomb dropped. My parents stopped me dead in my tracks, telling me they didn't approve of the topics I spoke about publicly.
>
> I was stunned and at first I didn't really know what to say. I recovered quickly, finding my voice, and responded, "Mom and Dad, I am forty-eight years old and

at this point in my life I really don't need your approval. You are entitled to your feelings. I believe that when I speak about what has happened to me personally, I open the door for others to feel they are not alone, and therefore I am going to continue because I am not ashamed of my life. If my story helps one person to not feel alone or to open up, then I know I have done my job."

After that conversation, I was at dinner with a very close friend one night discussing how I felt disconnected to my last name, Stern, because I felt it was angry, rigid, and strict, none of which I wanted to be. She brilliantly stated, "Why don't you drop your last name and use your middle name instead?" I had never even thought about that. In fact, I never even used my middle name. As I thought about it further, after dinner that night, I decided that's exactly what I was going to do. The next day I changed ALL my profiles on the web, got new business cards, and started going by Bonnie Gayle.

Based on the numbers, Bonnie Stern was a dictator-like energy and Bonnie Gayle was a heartfelt healer. After hearing that, I knew I was exactly who I was supposed to be. It took me forty-eight years to get there and I'm so grateful I did! As they say, "everything happens for a reason."

Another great example that involves the use of a nickname or self-imposed label came from one of my clients who is a coach.

Her friend and client named Graham always identified himself as "it's only Graham":

> With each phone call or voice mail message, my friend Graham would consistently add the word "only" or "just" to his identity. Over time, amongst our circle he became known as "only Graham," differentiating him from any other Graham. Who needs last names when this Graham added his own prefix of unworthiness? Each time he minimized his existence by emphasizing "only" or "just," he limited his size, importance, and value to himself, to others, and in the world, as if he sighed the smallness of his being.
>
> Reaching my breaking point of witnessing Graham's lack of confidence, I stuck my foot in in ways you can with friends when the timing feels "right." Okay, so the coach in me spoke a little more emphatically than the average friend might, but I did so with loving compassion. He got my point. Within days, he began stumbling at first to catch himself in his "only-ness" and "just-ness." He checked every time these words touched his lips, even when they were used to describe something unrelated to him. For a while he cut them off completely, as if nothing could be "only" or "just." To this day, he still raises an eyebrow when he hears anyone use these words, in secret celebration of his refreshed deserve-ability.

Graham's transformation of confidence all these years later is remarkable: his professional success, his healthy romantic relationship, and his role as a loving father. Yet, subtle to those who know him well, what is most impressive is his solid posture. He walks more up-right, claiming each stride as his own. His broad smile and wide eyes welcoming the world toward him, and leaving "only" and "just" in his wake.

In this case, Graham added the prefix or label of "only," but what does this word add to, or rather subtract from, his energy? "Only" adds to 21 and reduces to 3 (2 + 1 = 3). In the negative, the 3 lends the energy of self-doubt, self-criticism, and indecisiveness. In essence, Graham was giving away his personal power by energetically telling others he wasn't worth their time. "Just," the other label he frequently used, adds the distrusting, skeptical, and loner qualities of the 7. In both cases, the labels weren't allowing him to own his personal power. If you recall from earlier chapters, the scientific definition of the law of attraction says when an electron lowers its frequency, it gives off or discharges energy. Through the law of attraction, Graham was manifesting situations and circumstances that facilitated the giving away or "discharging" of his personal power. When he dropped the negative labels "only" and "just," he stopped lowering his frequency by discharging his personal power.

COINCIDENCE OR INTUITION?

Is it just a coincidence that these labels were chosen and that their dictionary meanings match exactly the vibrations they hold on an energetic level? Or is it that when we choose a name, title, or label, we are intuitively sensing the energetic patterns flowing within and around us?

Now that you've read through some examples, check it out for yourself! It's time to examine your own world for the various names, titles, and labels you encounter in your own life. Make a list of the most common ones you use and flip back to the word conversion chart in chapter 3 to decipher their energetic frequency to reveal what impact they may be having in your life. If you find that any of them are working through negative energy, it may be time to drop that label and choose a positive one. Dig a little deeper with them if necessary; as in the example of "peace" above, examine the two-digit sum before reducing it to a single digit. This allows you to see what other vibrations the word or label carries, giving you a crystal-clear energetic definition.

A good place to start this process would be to analyze any nicknames or pet names you apply to yourself or your loved ones. Do you call your daughter "princess" or your friend "pal"? It's time to take a closer look at what these and the other labels in your life are adding to (or subtracting from) your energy within and around you. Additionally, it would be good to also understand the effect those labels have on the people and things to which you are applying these labels. Your ability to positively creative the life you envision for yourself depends on understanding the effects of the words you assign to yourself and your surroundings.

CHAPTER 10

Advanced Words

THE THREE ENERGETIC COMPONENTS OF A WORD

Back in chapter 3, "Determining the Vibration of a Word through the Language of Numbers," we briefly discussed how words can be working with up to three energies or frequencies. For example, "hate" is the 16/7 vibration, "love" is 18/9, and "truth" is 27/9. Examining these additional energies can reveal much more about the frequency the word holds and more precisely details how you can work with it. Although the main essence (final sum reduced to a single digit) of a word is the most important energy, the sum before reducing to a single digit can further direct you in terms of whether the word has a natural tendency to be more positive or negative.

Using the word "hate" for example, which adds to 16/7, carries the 1, 6, and 7 energies within its makeup. The outer number (1) is the word's greatest strength (positive) and the inner number (6) is its greatest weakness (negative).

"Hate" is a very volatile change energy, and not just because the main essence of the word is the truth-seeker number 7. The inner and outer numbers paint a more detailed picture of why this word is energetically stripping. The word's greatest strength is the 1, the isolated, driven, pioneering number and the first physical-plane number. It seeks to form a separation or isolate you from whatever you are saying "hate" to or about.

The greatest weakness of "hate" is the 6, number of the creative visionary and the nurturer. The inner or weaker number is usually a reflection of the more negative energies the word is carrying. If it is a negative word, the inner number represents the negative energy (negative side of the number); in the case of a more positive word, the inner number shows that the negative energies of the number are less dominant or subdued in the weaker position, highlighting that it has less effect on the word than the outer number or greatest strength energy.

"Hate" is typically a negative word, so the 6 is expressing its negative side, being in the inner (or weaker) position. It also shows the potential to access the bigger picture creative-visionary energy (positive side of the 6) upon which the word could draw, transmuting its negative punch.

To pull this together, here are the definitions of all three of the energetic parts of a word:

Greatest strength (outer number): What a word is mainly utilizing to express through its main-essence number. In the case of "hate," although its main essence is a 7, the 1 as the greatest-strength number highlights the perspective through which it is viewed.

Greatest weakness (inner number): In the case of a negative word, the inner number represents the energy it could be utilizing to bring balance. In the case of a positive word, the inner number represents the subdued negative energy, giving favor to the highlighted outer number or greatest-strength energy.

Main essence (sum of all numbers reduced to single digit): The main or base energetic frequency of a word. It is the most important vibration as it represents a word's greatest impact. Think of the greatest-strength and greatest-weakness numbers as accessories or additional energies that work with the main-essence number, enhancing or detracting from it.

Now that you have the definitions of the inner, outer, and main-essence energies, below is the summary of the word "hate" as shown with all three of the numerical components that make up the word's vibration.

Hate

Greatest strength: The pioneering, overachieving, isolated, aggressive, self-absorbed number 1.

Greatest weakness: The balanced, nurturing, peace-making, optimistic, and creative visionary 6.

Main essence: The wise, philosophical, truth-seeking, and teaching/learning number 7.

"Hate" is strongly working through the 1; its greatest weakness is the need to add in some of the positive qualities of the 6 to balance out the isolated, over-driven, and selfish 1 energy.

Let's look at "love" next to see what further information we can reveal about this powerful word.

LOVE

Greatest strength: The pioneering, verbally self-expressive, new
   beginnings 1 energy.

Greatest weakness: The subdued independent, selfish, and
   detached 8 in the negative.

Main essence: The selfless, idealistic, and responsible humanitarian 9.

"Love" is working through the pioneering, verbally self-expressive 1 as the greatest-strength number with the independent, selfish, and detached 8 as the subdued greatest-weakness energy to create the selfless, idealistic, and responsible humanitarian as the base energy. The 9 is also the number representing both the beginning and end of a cycle or the number of completion. The phrase "love is all there is" makes perfect sense after analyzing the word's energetic vibrations.

In the negative, "love" could possibly turn selfish, dominating, and detached if the word was drawing out the negative 8 qualities it carries. Of course, this depends on how the word is used. The golden rule with any word is that there aren't any strictly positive or negative words but each has a positive and negative side and you get to choose which side you want to use.

Last but not least, let's reveal the deeper truth about "truth."

TRUTH

Greatest strength: The intuitive, supportive, cooperative, sensitive, and harmonious 2.

Greatest weakness: The impatient, impractical, self-absorbed, instant-gratification-seeking 4.

Main essence: The creative visionary (sees the bigger picture), nurturing, and optimistic 6.

"Truth" is gentle and intuitively sensitive with the 2 as its greatest strength. To know the truth is to reveal the deeper meaning through the intuitive energy of the 2. "Truth's" greatest weakness is the impatient, impractical, and selfish 4. In the subdued or weaker position, it stresses that the negative 4 qualities have a lesser effect on the word. To reveal truth often takes patience and progress, which is the 4 in a positive tone.

The main essence of "truth" is the creative visionary 6, allowing "truth" to see the bigger or broader picture but in a nurturing and optimistic way. In the negative, "truth" can be pessimistic, whiny, doubtful, critical, and fraught with worries and anxieties. "Tell me the truth!" is a phrase used when "truth" is being used in a demanding and critical way through the negative 6 qualities.

Let's take a look at some of the other ways names, labels, and titles can be presented and how energetically significant they can be.

THE PURE ENERGIES

Occasionally you'll come across a smaller word that only has a single-digit sum or a sum that is considered a "pure" energy, like the 30/3 for example. The pure 30/3 frequency is only working the number 3 because 0 is a symbol rather than a number; the role of the zero is to emphasize the impact of the 3 energy. Zero (0) represents the infinite or spiritual awareness, highlighting the purity and depth of the inspirational and imaginative 3. The pure numbers have more of a one-track focus. Often words that vibrate to a pure energy are either strictly positive or strictly negative with not much gray area. "Serene" is a pure 30/3 energy and it is either drawing power from the positive, inspirational, sensitive, and unifying 3 to create a serene existence, or the negative, self-doubting, self-critical, and indecisive 3, never truly allowing serenity to manifest.

The pure words that are working just one frequency are typically some of the most powerfully positive; when possible, incorporate them into your daily vocabulary to give your manifesting power a boost.

The reference chart at the back of the book, "Top Positive and Negative Words," gives the main essence definitions for these most-common words and phrases. When you pick your favorite words to add to your new-and-improved personal vernacular list, examine each word more closing by looking at all three of the numbers it works with.

The Master-Number Frequencies

Words that add to the master numbers (10/1, 11/2, 22/4, and 33/6) hold special significance as these frequencies are associated with the guiding roles and are considered by most numerological systems to have a greater energetic impact and significance.

The 10/1 combines the energies of the first physical-plane number (1) with the symbol of the infinite or spiritual awareness (0), reducing down to the trailblazing and driven 1. The 11/2 is the highest spiritual number and referred to as the spiritual-guide energy comprised of the verbally self-expressive and pioneering double 1 with the supportive, peaceful, and harmonious 2 as the base vibration. The 22/4 is the master-builder number, combining the gentle, supportive, and peaceful double 2 with the base energy of the solid, stable, foundation-building 4.

Lastly, the 33/6 is the master-teacher number, made up of a double dose of the inspirational, imaginative, and optimistic 3 and reducing to the creative-visionary 6 as the core energy.

When a word's numerical sum equals one of these master-number frequencies, it is ideal to view them with all three of their numbers intact. As always, the base number is the most important, but a word that adds to a master number is likely to add extra positive energetic power in whatever way you use it.

Brand Power

Branding is all the rage when it comes to leaving your mark in the twenty-first-century business world. Most branding companies advertise their services with the pitch that consistency in branding is everything, and if you don't have a strong brand, success will never be yours. There may be some truth to that statement, as the name or label you use for your personal or business name may make or break you in terms of attracting customers.

Coca-Cola is a brand that has endured for many decades and continues to hold strong in the marketplace. Why? Its label is energetically strong and people resonate with it because Coca-Cola has matched the message it presents with its name. Coca-Cola adds to 26/8, which is made up of the number of intuition (2) and the creative-visionary number (6), combining to form the number of independence and wisdom (8). Coca-Cola's slogan has always enforced a refreshing, invigorating, satisfying, feel-good message, keeping in alignment with the underlying energetic message of confidence, independence, and strength of the 8 vibration.

If you work in business or a professional industry where your name is spoken or used often (in business cards, documents, signage), it is a reflection of your brand or how your potential clients/customers might see you. In chapter 3, we touched on names and the different combinations, such as first names, last names, and full birth names, and we addressed what these mean on an energetic level. Let's take a look at your professional name, which represents your career life. Is your business or professional name drawing customers in or driving them away?

Celebrities often change their name to match the image or stage presence they want to achieve. One of my clients, celebrity stylist Carrie White, changed her name from Carole well before she was ever well known for her work. Never having liked her birth name, in her teen years she decided to go by Carrie because it felt right to her. On some level, she knew she was Carrie, and she was right. Although "Carole" and "Carrie" add to the same base number 9, they are very different versions of the nine. If you remember from chapter 3, the most important energy of a word is the base number, which is calculated by summing all the converted letters in a word to numbers and reducing them to a single digit. However, examining the sum of the digits before reducing to a single digit can give even more insight into the particulars of a word's frequency and the effects it has. Think of it as combining colors; if we mix red and blue, it makes purple, but the shade of purple we create depends on the shades of red and blue we're working with. "Carole" is a 27/9 and "Carrie" is a 36/9. "Carole" and "Carrie" are different "shades" of 9, the number of ambition, idealism, and responsibility. The 9 has a strong leadership air to it, but what kind of leaders are "Carole" and "Carrie"?

"Carrie" is a far more suitable name from an energetic standpoint in terms of her career and attracting success. For "Carole," the intuitive, sensitive, cooperative, and harmonious 2 leads. "Carrie" leads with the inspirational, imaginative, social-butterfly 3. The 2 is a great name vibration if you are, for example, a librarian; if you're aiming to be a celebrity stylist, the bright, sunny and social 3 energy is the way to go.

CITIES, STATES, AND COUNTRIES

Even the word vibration of the city, state, or country where you live can have an energetic influence. The United States of

America has been the hub of the world economy for decades. The full country name vibrates to the solid, stable, enduring, progressive, foundation number 4. In the more physical sense, 4 is materialistic and self-absorbed, so those seeking wealth and affluence often set sail for the United States of America in hopes of a better way of life through financial abundance.

Another variation of the United States of America is "USA." This is used more often than the former, and for good reason. The "USA" has long been considered "the land of the free"; on an energetic level, that's the message being transmitted with "USA." Even the last line of the national anthem states this message: "O'er the land of the free and the home of the brave!" "USA" resonates with the compassionate, heart-centered, erratic, and freedom-of-expression number 5. In the land of the free, you have the freedom to express yourself. On the flip side, 5 in the negative is detached and power-hungry, which may explain why the USA has held its position as the leader of the world for long.

India has been home to many spiritual gurus and is commonly known as the "land of spirituality." Indeed it is, even on an energetic level. The word "India" holds the frequency of the 10, a master number for the earth-guide energy. Combining the pioneering, isolated, achievement-based, first physical-plane 1 with the 0 symbol of the infinite or spiritual awareness shows why the country has shared such a vast amount of spiritual wisdom with the world through its teachers, gurus, and texts. The word "India" brings spiritual wisdom (0) into the physical (1).

To spice things up, let's look at a city that doesn't exist anymore but still continues to hold mystery and intrigue thousands of years after its supposed demise. The lost city of Atlantis is believed to have been home to an advanced civilization that existed, according to the information contained within the writings of the Greek philosopher Plato, approximately 11,000 years ago but was destroyed by a cataclysmic event in 9000 BCE. There may be a reason why Atlanteans are believed to have been highly advanced. The lost civilization was said to have advanced technologies and knowledge far ahead of the time period when it existed. The name "Atlantis" holds the energy of the creative visionary 6. Could it be that the city's name vibration allowed those residing there to harness the visionary "bigger picture" energy of the 6 vibration to advance rapidly ahead of their time?

Among my more spiritual clients, I have found over the past couple of years that more people are being drawn to the state of California for both work and play. The word "California" vibrates to the base frequency of 7, the truth-seeker number. At a time when the world's financial structures are crumbling and the corporations are being exposed as corrupt, it seems many people are gravitating to places that resonate with truth and integrity to find a sense of inner balance. Having traveled to many cities, provinces, and states in North America over the years, I can account for the fact that even the vibration of a place's name can affect the people living in it. For example, New York City is known for its fashion-conscious crowd; New York City is a 6, the number of creativity, creative expression, and being the visionary. Los Angeles, which is also the home of Hollywood and the TV and movie industries, is a 10. The 10 combines the energies of the pioneering, trailblazing 1 with the spiritually aware 0. The 10 holds adaptable energy, but also likes to keep life fun and light, preferring to have a good time over dealing with serious matters.

It's worth noting the energies corresponding with the names of the country, state or province, and city where you live to understand the vibrations those words are adding to or subtracting from your energy. When you travel, do you feel more alive in other cities than your current state or city? Based on your goals and dreams, a city that vibrates to a practical and foundation-building 4 may not be a good fit for someone who likes to live life with spontaneity and always searching out freedom of expression.

Naming Intangible Objects

Do you call your car "Bessie" or the "Ol' Jalopy"? If you're the kind of person who likes to slap a name or label on intangible things, from cars to remote controls, what is that energetic shift infusing into your environment? If you tend to have more car trouble than the average person, maybe it's time to stop calling the car "Bessie," which vibrates with the erratic, free-flowing, and unpredictable 5 energy.

It's a common occurrence to name a boat or yacht. The frequency the name or label holds can affect the experiences of those who enjoy the boat. The *Titanic* sank on its maiden voyage, and the boat's name quite possibly could have had an effect on the tragedy, influencing those on the boat including the captain and his crew. "Titanic" vibrates to the number 31/4. Note that the inspirational, optimistic, imaginative, mental-based 3 is at the helm with this name and the pioneering, trailblazing, and driven physical-based 1 is in the weaker position. The base energy of the word is the practical, solid-foundation number 4, but this particular arrangement of the 4 (31/4) tends to be more impractical, being led by the overly optimistic, social-butterfly 3. It seems the *Titanic* would have benefited from a more practical and enduring 4 name.

Naming intangible items can have an influence on you, even though it is not part of your main essence. These inanimate objects affect your outer-environment energies and how you view these items. Essentially, these labels are shaping your beliefs or opinions, and in doing so, are shaping what you manifest.

Different Languages

The letters in a word can be compared to musical notes on a music sheet. Each musical note has its own set tone or vibration, and regardless of your native tongue, notes on a music sheet will sound the same when interpreted and played. Similarly, the "notes," or letters, in a word have a set tone or vibration no matter the language with which it is deciphered.

According to the biblical scriptures, Hebrew is considered to be the first language that was used by God when creating the world. Many languages have evolved throughout the centuries, yet English, which is not even the most-spoken language in the world, is quickly becoming the global language. With English-speaking countries at the hub of global commerce and the entertainment and media industries, there is a growing need to learn functional English in order to stay abreast of the current business world.

This book is based on the English language and the corresponding alphabet, but the methods in this book can be used in other languages as well. Words often do not mean the same thing in all cultures and languages; because two words in different languages might contain different letters, a word will vibrate to a different frequency depending on the language from which it is translated. If you speak other languages regularly, it is definitely worth your while to calculate the frequency of those words as well, to see what you may be manifesting with them.

For example, in Hebrew, the word "love" is considered to be a very special word; it not only means something different in the Hebrew culture than it does in Westernized cultures, it also adds to a different numerical sum and has a different energetic influence. The reference section in the back of this book tells us that "love" in English adds to a 9, the number representing both the beginning and end of a cycle and humanitarian energy; in the negative, it can be judgmental and critical. Think unconditional (positive 9) or conditional (negative 9) love. Alternatively, the Hebrew version of love is *ahava*, a two-part word that means "I give" and "I love." "Ahava" is the 6 energy, the creative-expression number, the visionary and nurturer.

In other languages, the definition can be the same, but the energetic meaning is different. The word "but" in English translates to *pero* in Spanish. Their dictionary meaning is the same, but the energetic vibration is a bit different. "But" is a pessimistic, critical, and judgmental 6 while "pero" is also a judgmental energy, but in the form of the critical, opinionated, and narrow-minded 9.

For many languages, you can match the English alphabet to find the numerical meaning of a word but there are some exceptions to watch for. For example, the Hebrew alphabet is alphanumeric: each Hebrew letter also has a numerical value and can be used as a number. When calculating a Hebrew word, it is best to use the Hebrew alphanumeric values to get the most accurate energetic definition. A Hebrew gematria conversion chart is best used in this case (see figure 1 on page 46).

If you are familiar with words or phrases in languages other than English and are curious about the words' energetic meanings in that form, go ahead and calculate their energetic meanings using a gematria chart similar to the one found in chapter 3. There are many available on the Internet for the purpose of various language conversions.

There are many well-known quotes from famous people like Hitler, Jesus, and Gandhi that have left lasting marks on the world through the power and context of the words they chose. Originally, some of these words were not spoken in English. Spoken in their original form, like any other translated vocabulary, the wording may or may not vary slightly when translated to the English meaning.

Below are some of these quotes and the quotes' main keyword meanings based on the English version:

"Hate is more lasting than dislike."—Adolf Hitler

Most would consider Adolf Hitler to be memorable for his unthinkable actions, but his words speak volumes about the perceptions he held of his world. The energetic goldmines in this phrase are "hate" and "dislike." Although Hitler's views may have been skewed drastically from the truth, this phrase is actually very true—hate is more lasting than dislike, literally and energetically. "Hate" is a 7 frequency; in the negative, it represents a deep-seated sense of distrust. "Dislike" is a 6 frequency; in the negative, like the word "war," it represents pessimism, criticism, and judgment. Energetically speaking, "hate" does have a stronger and more lasting impression than "dislike," as pessimistic thinking can be more easily changed than a deep-seated sense of distrust.

"Everyone who seeks, finds."—Jesus

"Seeks" and "finds" are the highlighted gems in this quote. "Seeks" is the 5 energy, the number of freedom of expression. "Finds" is the 7, the deep and philosophical truth-seeker energy. There is certainly a deeper meaning here other than just stating the fact that if we seek, we will find. When we are free to express our uniqueness (5), we will find our truth (7). This truly is the essence or purpose of our existence, as we are all in search of our own truth, not the truth of anyone else. Although we will all find a different truth (7), it will be the right version of truth for us if we are free to express our unique expression (5).

"A man is but the product of his thoughts; what he thinks, he becomes."—Mahatma Gandhi

The igniting words in this phrase are "thinks" and "becomes." "Thinks" vibrates to the 9, the number of idealism, which goes perfectly with this word's dictionary definition of "to have or formulate in the mind." "Becomes" resonates with the 8, the number of confidence, independence, and wisdom. This statement energetically impresses upon us that we are independently responsible for creating our reality via the thoughts we hold.

The current English alphabet is based on the Latin alphabet, like the German and Swedish languages that also have twenty-six-letter alphabets (based on the Latin version), both of which can be easily and directly converted to English. Even Mandarin and Japanese can be converted to the English letter combination equivalent using widely available conversion charts.

A letter has an unchanging frequency and many languages can be matched precisely letter for letter. When this is not possible, it is important to remember that a significant part of language is our individual interpretation of it. Like the example of the word "love" in English and in Hebrew, the word means something a bit different in each of those languages, but depending on your culture, upbringing, and personal views, it can be just the right meaning for you. When converting words to their numerical equivalent, regardless of the language, the most important influence is the meaning of a word to the person using it. The wisest words spoken are meaningless in a language not understood by the listener.

The energetic meaning of a word is only a part of the complete picture when it comes to utilizing the power of language. When working with energy, it's our choice as to how we use it. We can choose to allow it to affect us in a positive or negative way, but our feelings and viewpoints of words can also be shaped by what we have learned from outside sources.

If you recall the reference in chapter 1 to the child learning to speak who repeats a profane word, the word is neutral to the child because the child holds no feeling or thought power behind the word. Likewise, if you have no knowledge of Mandarin, Spanish, or Portuguese, these languages will have very little if any energetic influence on you.

If you speak more than one language, it is necessary for you to explore your vocabulary from an energetic standpoint in all languages in order to gain a complete understanding of what you are creating in your life through the words you use. Even if you don't speak another language, it can be fun to explore other languages as a means of better understanding the perspective of our global community. English, Chinese, German, Spanish, and African countries vary greatly in cultural experience. Could the different languages and the vibrational influences they have be a factor in our global diversity? As English gains in popularity throughout many cultures, will we see a shift toward a more unified view via the vibration of language?

CHAPTER 11

Star-Studded Word Power

What separates us from the rich and famous? Is it just luck, fate, chance, or is there an element that we could all tap into in order to access that same level of abundance and success? The celebrity lives we glimpse on TV, with their ever-flowing abundance, seem a million miles away from our own realities. What's their secret?

Based on my experience of working with many successful business owners, celebrities, and other elite professionals, their secret isn't a secret at all. The magic happens from the perception they create of themselves through the words they choose to use. Take Donald Trump, for example; despite his outdated appearance, his presence demands respect and admiration from those around him. Have you ever noticed that wealthy people have no trouble asking to be compensated for what they feel they're worth?

This chapter illustrates that successful people have perfected the skill of manifesting abundance in their lives, but also shows that it wasn't always this way for them. Most often, they've had to change the negative patterns in their thoughts and actions just like the rest of us, suggesting that there really isn't such a thing as an overnight success. You get what you put into life, and that includes putting effort into your vocabulary. Words are our primary means of communicating with others; what we think, speak, or write can instantly change our connection with someone or even the trajectory of our life, as these stories vividly highlight.

CARRIE WHITE, CELEBRITY STYLIST

With a posh Beverly Hills salon, having styled the likes of Elvis Presley, Brad Pitt, and Sandra Bullock (to name a few), Carrie White is manifesting abundance into her life. On the day I first met Carrie White, she was exactly who I envisioned a Hollywood hairstylist to be: beautiful, elegant, and classy. She seemed to have it together in every way, but at the end of our session, she handed a copy of her book, *Upper Cut*, to me, and my vision of her was forever changed. I fully expected to find a book filled with superficial stories of Hollywood parties and celebrity secrets, but what I found within those pages was downright shocking.

Carrie had a dark backstory tainted with sexual abuse, abandonment, alcoholism, drug addiction, and attempted recoveries. She had lived the equivalent of three lifetimes in one, and much of it wasn't the glitz and glam you'd expect in a Hollywood stylist's life portfolio. She had climbed to success, came crashing down to rock bottom, and then climbed back up again. What saved her and brought her back from the brink of failure and tragedy? Fate, luck, sheer determination, or was there something more at work?

Many things in Carrie's memoir stood out for me that confirmed she was a fighter and a trailblazer, but one of the key phrases she used often throughout those years was, "Of course! That's my specialty." That phrase, if viewed from the surface, seemed insignificant and actually more of a little white lie; however, it was actually a powerful manifestation tool that opened doors for her. Even when she knew nothing about what she was about to do for a client, she would confidently announce this phrase. These words were pivotal in gaining respect and admiration from clients and colleagues and eventually gaining the self-respect she needed to own her gifts and talents and achieve lasting success:

> It was a magical phrase that set me up for confidence with a moment to pause and think things through, because after I said it, there were no more probing questions. People just become quiet and say "Oh!"—kinda stunned, and let me have the upper hand on the subject.
>
> The next great thing for me is that this was an exercise of pushing my envelope to improve, be better, and make an expert out of myself, forcing me to do an excellent job without excuses, because of course I had to. "It" was my specialty, so I better be good, and I razzled and dazzled and made it happen. It has been a psychological plus for all concerned.

Carrie's story is a "fake it 'til you make it" scenario. You might feel as though you don't know where to begin because the positive words you've chosen for your new Top Ten Power Words list just don't fit your reality—yet. Like Carrie did, you can fake it until they DO fit. By using that phrase, Carrie helped shape the vision of the stylist she truly was but had yet to fully blossom into.

In Carrie's star-studded word-power example, the key phrase is "of course." This phrase from a dictionary standpoint is infused with a matter-of-fact, confident, and assertive undertone. Energetically, "of course" is the number of imagination, inspiration, and unity. The optimistic, the-sky's-the-limit, imaginative power of the 3 and its unifying, connect-the-dots kind of energy allowed Carrie to erase any doubts and wholeheartedly believe that she could do it.

Steve Allen, Founder and Owner of Steve Allen Media

I first met Steve Allen at a cafe in Los Angeles. A mutual friend had previously introduced us, and as I walked toward his table, he looked the part of a publicist (with a tailored suit and all). When I sat down across from him, I saw a spark in his eyes that I'll never forget. After I got to know Steve, I understood what that spark was all about. He's not a typical publicist; he is such an out-of-the-box thinker that his ideas can seem outrageous at first, but I'm convinced he's a creative genius. He uses words like "talkaboutable" and "get eyeballed," and is one of the most enthusiastic and inspirational people I've met.

Steve started out as an actor in the Big Apple with a variety of roles, including having played the "father of the ugly baby" on *Seinfeld*. After getting married, he moved to Los Angeles and decided to dabble in public relations to support his growing family. His new business venture grew, but it wasn't until his wife came up with the tagline "PR with a conscience" that the magic began to happen. The words "PR" and "conscience" aren't normally used together in the same sentence, but for Steve, it's a perfect fit. He's real in every way, and the monetary rewards are secondary to a job well done.

Steve now owns one of the most successful PR agencies in the US with bicoastal offices in both Los Angeles and New York. His success is obviously attributed in part to his hard-working and inventive outlook, but there's no denying that his tagline, "PR with a conscience," is a powerful energetic representation of what Steve Allen is all about. It isn't just a catchy tagline; he lives and breathes it every day:

> It's funny; you own and run a company, and because of that you know you have a responsibility to your employees and company clients to express a feeling, or statement, or expression, something besides your company name, something to clearly express to others what your company is all about. Anyway, I toyed with creating a tagline after our company name for numerous months. I needed something to put on our website, letterhead, news releases, etcetera—something that hollered the essence of Steve Allen Media. One night, during dinner, my wife looked at me and said, "How's this for a tagline

after Steve Allen Media: 'PR with a conscience.'" That was it; the search was over, and the team all voted. It was unanimous. Everyone felt it. Our company had been defined. We lived by that tagline, we cared, we told the truth, and we wanted clients who wanted to make a difference in our world. That happened over five years ago, and the tagline is still the way we all operate at Steve Allen Media. Life is good.

Steve's business name was an instant hit for him, even on an unseen level. The keywords in his business name are "PR" and "conscience." These are the words most often remembered when someone speaks or reads his company's name, and therefore they have the most energetic power. "PR" is a 7, the deep, philosophical, and truth-seeking energy. "Conscience" is a 9, the ambitious, idealistic, responsible, humanitarian number. Together these words have a profound energetic effect on someone by saying his PR firm is a truth-centered humanitarian-based company.

RICKY POWELL, NBC DIRECTOR AND THE HAPPINESS GUY

Ricky Powell has been in the entertainment industry for most of his life. He began as a child star in commercials and in guest appearances on shows like *Sabrina the Teenage Witch*. He moved on to work for the media giant, NBC. A mutual friend connected us, and when we met for the first time, I didn't expect to find such a smiling, happy-go-lucky guy sitting at the restaurant table. Most of the media people I've met were anything but happy people, but instead typically tended to be hardened by the negative nature of the industry. Ricky Powell wasn't anything like that. I was skeptical at first that his "happiness" was just a part of his platform to brand himself as "the Happiness Guy," but throughout our conversation that day, I realized he truly was happy because he *chose* to be happy. Instead of viewing his situation as hopeless and helpless, working in a career that could leave him ultimately feeling empty inside, he decided to create his own happiness by changing his perspective on his life through the power of words:

> Words have made quite an amazing difference in my life. Although it has been said that words account for only a small percentage of your overall message when communicating with others, while your tone of voice and body language account for the vast majority, I strongly believe this is only part of the equation.
>
> What I believe is even more important than the words you use to convey your message with the outside world is the inner power words have on you as your words directly affect your mind, thoughts, actions, and your life.
>
> In our culture, we are bombarded with so many negative messages every day with our different forms of media—plus what we see and hear right in our daily lives—not to mention the quiet but sometimes destructive little inner voice serving as our own worst critic.
>
> As Earl Nightingale once said, "You become what you think about," most of the time. Until I became a

student and then a teacher of happiness, I was one of those people who wasn't happy because I didn't think about happy things, especially due to the fact that I had devoted my entire life to media and the entertainment industry.

Once I learned how impactful our thoughts and our words can be, I made a conscious effort to rearrange my patterns and began specifically using words that would empower my life rather than derail it. Words like "abundance," "achieve," "affirm," "beauty," "bliss," "bountiful," "considerate," "cooperate," "courageous," and of course the list goes on and on. You get the idea. The secret is not only in the words we use with others, but in the words we use inside our minds and our hearts.

Make sure you are building yourself up with your words, allowing your mind to create the exact reality you are dreaming about. You can do it easily and systematically; you just need to decide you won't settle for anything less.

The driving words behind Ricky's catchphrase he created for himself are "happiness" and "guy." What does it truly mean to be "the Happiness Guy"? Energetically, this title is raw and real. It holds the frequency of 7, like the word "hate" (see chapter 10); however, "Happiness Guy" is the positive, truth-seeking, deep, and philosophical 7, highlighting that we must live our truth to be truly happy. To be truly happy, we must discover and live our truth as Ricky has, even in the midst of unhappiness. Using this title, Ricky not only represents his own path and what he did in his own life to find happiness, but he also sends out the energetic message that he can help others find their own truth and begin living it as well.

Treva Etienne, Actor and Director

I first met Treva Etienne on a radio show where I did a live numerological profile on him. He was not only my first official celebrity client, it was also the start of a very special and pivotal friendship for me—one I didn't expect to happen. After the radio interview, Treva called me to thank me for the reading and to say how accurate and insightful it was for him. I could sense his genuineness and we ended the conversation by saying we would keep in touch. I knew it wasn't just a nicety; he meant what he said.

We have indeed kept in touch over the years, and it is a friendship I value greatly. One of the things I admire about him is his belief that we each need to live our truth, not anyone else's, in order to be truly happy and content. Although Treva has had a multitude of roles in major motion pictures, television shows, and commercials over the years and is an accomplished actor and director, he has always been firm in his outlook that he refused to step outside what he feels is true to him in order to succeed. Many Hollywood stars sell their souls to make it on the big screen. Yet Treva is a perfect example of how living in alignment with what feels right to you will always get you to exactly where you need to be in life, whether it is by the actions you take or the words you choose to speak. No compromises necessary:

"What doesn't kill you makes you stronger" has followed me all my life. I have been in challenging situations where that phrase has propelled me to keep moving onward and don't look back to slow me down.

A few years back, I sold a TV comedy show to a new network that was looking for a new comedy idea like mine. I was brought in to create my production team, cast the show with comedians, and work on the pilot. If they liked the pilot and the network gave the green light, I was to do thirteen episodes. I shot the pilot and everyone loved it, so I was set to shoot the full thirteen. Instead, I discovered that the production company and my hand-picked producer had conspired to compensate another director to whom the production company owed money. They gave the other director the thirteen-episode job and told me that I wasn't good enough. This news—two days before Christmas—was devastating, and I felt the betrayal of my friend whom had agreed to keep the news from me in order to keep her producer job that I had fought hard to get for her.

"What doesn't kill you makes you stronger" kept going through my head. I believed in myself, and I went on to win a best short film award with HBO and another best short film award at the Hollywood Scarefest film festival for another film I wrote and directed.

I continue to live my life with that phrase and share it with friends and people I meet who forget they always have the power, strength, and choice to keep moving forward and believe in their destiny.

As you can see, through all of the amazing examples in this chapter of star-studded word power, the rich and famous are just like the rest of us, creating what they desire in the exact same way. No matter who you are or what your list of accomplishments might be, the words you choose to think, speak, and write have a powerful influence on your life, moment by moment, and they are constantly shaping your destiny.

The key words in the phrase "what doesn't kill you makes you stronger" are "kill" and "stronger." Even though they are opposing words based on their dictionary meanings, "kill" and "stronger" are both 8 frequencies. However, like Ricky's example above, these two words add to the truth-seeker number 7 (8 + 8 = 16 and 1 + 6 = 7). Those double 8 wisdom-filled words combine to allow Treva to find the deeper, more significant truth in his experiences through the 7 energy. It urged him to look beyond the superficial to the greater picture or deeper truth inherent in the situation and his life.

Conclusion

That's a wrap, folks! You now have all the tools, knowledge, and steps to change your life using the energy of words. The goal of the book was to create a more mindful view of the words you choose to use based on the knowledge that they can also influence what you create and how. The words you use are creating and shaping your reality moment by moment; choose them wisely.

The power of words and their profound ability to shape our destiny is often the most overlooked, yet is one of the most vital pieces in consistently and successfully applying the law of attraction. If your life isn't going the way you imagined it to be, look no further for the solution than the words you use every day. The golden rule of the energetic world is that all things are energy, including words. Think of energy as a medium you can mold and shape as you desire. Each word has a positive and negative side, yet there are no "good" or "bad" words—only positive or negative vibrations. How you choose to use those vibrations—whether thought, spoken, or written—is the deciding factor in what you want to create in your world. Remember, it is as much the word vibrations themselves as it is the energy and feeling you put behind them. If you focus on the negative side of a word, your life will reflect that negativity on some level.

The recommended reading section at the end of the book will get you started on the journey. But for the information in this book to truly work manifesting magic in your life, you'll want to add your personal style and flavor by creating your own unique list using the word conversion chart in chapter 3. Use notebook or folder to keep all your word lists in the same place for easy reference. Like any transformational program, it has to resonate with you or you won't stick with it to create lasting change. Your success boils down to what you believe to be true in your world. Words can have all the power or none of it, depending on the energy you give them. The choice is all yours.

As you take inventory of your words and exchange some or all for new ones, remember that some things are just meant to be, especially when it comes to names and labels. Go with your gut in the end, even if a name or label vibration appears not to be a match for you on an energetic level. It may be that you need that name for various "hidden" reasons or to accomplish an important life lesson. You might never know the full reason behind why you need certain words or labels in your life, but you can go with how you feel about it. As I always say, if it feels good, do it! Aim for your gut to be the driving force behind changing any words in your vocabulary. Manifesting in the positive is supposed to feel good. Life is meant to be enjoyed, so have fun on your word journey and happy manifesting!

Top Positive and Negative Words

This section lists some of the words that changed the minds of many throughout history. You now have them at your fingertips, and you are able to use them to shape your own life as you wish. This section is meant to serve two functions: 1) to help you rewrite your personal jargon list in the positive, and 2) to act as a reference or guide going forward.

The positive word list contains fewer examples in the word descriptions than the negative words list, as imagining and creating is easier with a positive word than a negative one, despite the fact that the average personal jargon list contains more negative words than positive. The following lists can be added to and expanded; there are many more positive and negative words in existence that might deserve some spotlight. Feel free to add to the lists or create one that is entirely your own. The words you choose to include in your daily life need to completely resonate with you in order to manifest the life you truly want.

TOP POSITIVE WORDS

Absolutely (6)

Meaning: "Absolutely" vibrates to the 6, the number of creativity, the nurturer, and the visionary. When used in the positive, "absolutely" produces a feeling of certainty with whatever it is used in reference to. The 6 affords the ability to see the bigger picture as connect-the-dots visionary energy. In the negative, as in "absolutely not," it can create feelings of judgment, pessimism, and criticism, which are the opposing traits of the creative visionary 6 vibration.

Positive: creative visionary, certainty, balanced, nurturing, peace-making, optimistic, and forward-thinking.

Negative: pessimistic, judgmental, critical, worrywart, people-pleasing, doubtful, and gossipy.

Abundant (8)

Meaning: "Abundant" vibrates to the 8, the number of wisdom, independence, confidence, and manifestation. As the most active soul-plane number and the energy of confidence, the 8 in the positive doesn't doubt, naturally allowing for the flow of abundance to come into our lives. In the negative, the 8 energy turns greedy, dominating, and selfish—not the kind of abundant energy that is sustaining and fulfilling long term.

Positive: wise, confident, assertive, independent, manifesting, assured, and loving.

Negative: detached, selfish, greedy, dominating, bossy, and attention-seeking.

Achieve (8)

Meaning: "Achieve" vibrates to the 8, the number of wisdom, independence, confidence, and manifestation. As the most active soul-plane number and the energy of confidence, 8 in the positive doesn't doubt, allowing you to achieve success readily and easily, believing wholeheartedly that you can achieve what you set out to accomplish. In the negative, "achieve" turns to the egocentric qualities of the 8, aiming to achieve a selfish, dominating, and greed-filled agenda.

Positive: wise, confident, assertive, independent, manifesting, assured, and loving.

Negative: detached, selfish, greedy, dominating, bossy, and attention-seeking.

Agree (9)

Meaning: "Agree" vibrates to the 9, the ambitious, idealistic, responsible, humanitarian number. The 9 is responsible for all the incredible achievements seen in the previous century as everyone had at least one 9 in their date of birth. The 9 is the most active mental number, the highest change vibration, and considered the "big dreamer." The black-and-white, right-and-wrong energy of the 9 gives "agree" its finality. When you "agree," you are making a decision; "I agree to side with you." In the negative, "agree" is more demanding, pulling from the opinionated and judgmental side of the 9; "I can't agree with you on that one, I just don't see it that way."

Positive: humanitarian, ambitious, responsible, justice-seeking, idealistic, and unselfish.

Negative: driven, opinionated, judgmental, critical, black and white, and narrow-minded.

Alive (4)

Meaning: "Alive" vibrates to the 4, the solid, stable, practical, and balanced foundation number. Considered the number of the "doer," it provides the word "alive" with the extra physical exertion to soar on all levels. To feel "alive" is to feel grounded in the physical, feeling capable of going after your goals and dreams. In the negative, 4 is materialistic and self-absorbed in the physical plane. Feeling "alive" then manifests in the negative side of the 4 as seeking gratifying physical activities like drugs, alcohol, sex, shopping, or other physical-based pleasures.

Positive: endurance, progress, foundation, practical, balanced, organization, solid, stable, and loyal.

Negative: materialistic, impatient, addictive, instant gratification, and self-absorbed.

Amaze (1)

Meaning: "Amaze" vibrates to the number 1, with the isolated pioneer, new beginnings, and trailblazing energy. The 1 is the only number not divisible by any other number, so it is a stand-alone energy. When we amaze through our actions, we do something that has not been done before, go above and beyond, or bring a new twist to the old. The word "amaze" has a "shock and awe" quality to it. In the negative, "amaze" turns to the negative and egocentric qualities of the 1, exhibiting the desire to be aggressive and attention-seeking in order to amaze.

Positive: verbal self-expression, initiate, action, ambitious, determined, and pioneering.

Negative: aggressive, egocentric, overly driven, self-absorbed, overachieving, and single-focused.

Attract (2)

Meaning: "Attract" vibrates to the 2, the number of intuition, sensitivity, and cooperation. The 2 is a dualistic energy and can "attract" in both the positive and the negative. When you attract from a negative standpoint, you utilize traits of the 2 and may be in a state of codependence, uncertainty, passivity, or hypersensitivity. From a positive stance, you attract from a balanced, cooperative, and intuitive place, drawing upon the positive side of the number 2 energy. Whether you are in a negative or positive state, you will attract more of that same state into your life in various ways, depending on the intentions you set.

Positive: balance, cooperation, sensitive, intuitive, supportive, and harmonious.

Negative: contrast, codependent, uncertain, submissive, passive, and hypersensitive.

Attraction (4)

Meaning: "Attraction" vibrates to the 4, the solid, stable, practical, and balanced foundation number. Considered the number of the "doer," the energy of the 4 is very physical-based, yet it is the same vibration the spiritual realm uses to permeate and manifest into the physical. "Attraction" happens energetically (e.g., the law of attraction) but appears as a physical effect; "It was an instant state of attraction between us." In the negative, "attraction" is even more physical-based, drawing upon the instant gratification-seeking and materialistic of the negative side of the 4.

Positive: endurance, progress, foundation, practical, balanced, organization, solid, stable, and loyal.

Negative: materialistic, impatient, addictive, instant gratification, and self-absorbed.

Begin (1)

Meaning: "Begin" vibrates to the number 1, with the isolated pioneer, new beginnings, and trailblazing energy. The 1 is the only number not divisible by any other number so it is a stand-alone energy. When you begin something new, it is the new beginnings or turn-the-page energy of the 1 that is filtering through; "I want to begin a new exercise routine next week." In the negative, "begin" takes on the driven, overachieving, and single-focused traits of the 1; "I must begin work on this project today, before someone on the team steals my idea."

Positive: verbal self-expression, initiate, action, ambitious, determined, and pioneering.

Negative: aggressive, egocentric, overly driven, self-absorbed, overachieving, and single-focused.

Believe (6)

Meaning: "Believe" vibrates to the 6, the number of creativity, the nurturer, and the visionary. Like the visionary 6 energy, when you positively believe in something, you envision yourself involved in whatever you believe in (you are able to see the bigger picture). In the negative, you are infusing the doubtful or pessimistic energy of the 6 and are skeptical of what you want to believe will actually happen or has happened; "I believe in you" or "I can't believe it."

Positive: creative visionary, certainty, balanced, nurturing, peace-making, optimistic, and forward-thinking.

Negative: pessimistic, judgmental, critical, worrywart, people-pleasing, doubtful, and gossipy.

Best (1)

Meaning: "Best" vibrates to the 1, with the isolated pioneer, new beginnings, and trailblazing energy. The 1 is the only number not divisible by any other number so it is a stand-alone energy. When you strive to be the "best" at anything, you take on the pioneering and hardworking energies of the number 1. In the negative, it changes to seeking to be the "best" in an aggressive, egocentric, and overachieving manner.

Positive: verbal self-expression, initiate, action, ambitious, determined, and pioneering.

Negative: aggressive, egocentric, overly driven, self-absorbed, overachieving, and single-focused.

Breakthrough (8)

Meaning: "Breakthrough" vibrates to the 8, the number of wisdom, independence, confidence, and manifestation. As the most active soul-plane number, 8 has a direct link to the spiritual realm, creating the knowing that comes from having a breakthrough experience; "I finally had a breakthrough; it came to me all of a sudden after weeks of trying to figure it out." In the negative, instead of a breakthrough being a profound and spiritual "aha" moment that happens to you without your intervention, the selfish, dominating, and bossy energies of the 8 attempt to force or create a breakthrough; "I'm going to be the one to have a breakthrough with this project if it's the last thing I do."

Positive: wise, confident, assertive, independent, manifesting, assured, and loving.

Negative: detached, selfish, greedy, dominating, bossy, and attention-seeking.

Brilliant (7)

Meaning: "Brilliant" vibrates to the 7, the deep, philosophical, teaching and learning number of truth-seeker energy. As the number of truth, "brilliant" gets its gifted, inspired, and radiant energy from revealing the truth through the positive 7; "That's brilliant, Sara! I can't believe you figured it out!" In the negative, the distrustful, hesitant, and skeptical energies of the 7 cast a shadow of doubt; "Oh no, not another one of your brilliant ideas."

Positive: wise, contemplative, achiever, truth-seeking, determined, and hands-on.

Negative: stubborn, overactive, distrustful, hesitant, skeptical, and loner.

Capable (4)

Meaning: "Capable" vibrates to the 4, the solid, stable, practical, and balanced foundation number. Considered the number of the "doer," it provides the word "capable" with the extra physical exertion to soar on all levels. To feel "capable" is to feel grounded in the physical, knowing you can achieve success with your goals and dreams. In the negative, "capable" is clouded by the impatient and instant gratification energy of the 4, casting doubts that you are "capable" and causing you to lose lasting momentum with your goals.

Positive: endurance, progress, foundation, practical, balanced, organization, solid, stable, and loyal.

Negative: materialistic, impatient, addictive, instant gratification, and self-absorbed.

Change (2)

Meaning: "Change" vibrates to the 2, the number of intuition, sensitivity, cooperation, and dualistic energy. When you embrace change, you are centered in the cooperative, harmonious, and intuitive side of the 2 energy. In the negative, you resist or oppose change by stepping into the codependent, uncertain, and contrasting side of the 2; "I can change anything I choose" or "I'll never overcome that obstacle to make the change."

Positive: balance, cooperation, sensitive, intuitive, supportive, and harmonious.

Negative: contrast, codependent, uncertain, submissive, passive, and hypersensitive.

Choice (7)

Meaning: "Choice" vibrates to the 7, the deep, philosophical, teaching and learning number of truth-seeker energy. When you make a choice, you draw up the wisdom and truth you have accumulated thus far to make a decision. As the truth-seeker number 7, "choice" is deciding the best truth for you and acting upon it. In the positive, you are confident in your choice because you are in alignment with your truth and inner wisdom, which does not doubt. When you doubt your truth, you are hesitant to make a choice and are in alignment with the negative side of the 7 vibration.

Positive: wise, contemplative, achiever, truth-seeking, determined, and hands-on.

Negative: stubborn, overactive, distrustful, hesitant, skeptical, and loner.

Clear (3)

Meaning: "Clear" vibrates to the 3, the intellectual number of imagination, memory, and inspiration. The 3 also represents unity or coming together. When you are clear about a choice or decision, you are pulling together in unity (3) all of your knowledge and wisdom you have accumulated about the choice or decision to become clear in your choice. In the negative, "clear" becomes clouded by the self-doubting, critical, and indecisive energy of the 3.

Positive: analytical, intelligent, humorous, social, sensitive, observant, unity, and inspirational.

Negative: critical, vain, grandeur, self-doubting, self-critical, overanalyzing, and indecisive.

Complete (8)

Meaning: "Complete" vibrates to the 8, the number of wisdom, independence, confidence, and manifestation. As the most active soul-plane number, 8 has a direct link to the spiritual realm, creating a sense of doubtlessness. When you feel whole and complete, there is no doubt present, as the feeling of completeness comes from a soul level within. In the negative, you seek to feel complete through outer means, utilizing the dominating and selfish energies of the 8.

Positive: wise, confident, assertive, independent, manifesting, assured, and loving.

Negative: detached, selfish, greedy, dominating, bossy, and attention-seeking.

Confidence (6)

Meaning: "Confidence" vibrates to the 6, the number of creativity, the nurturer, and the visionary. When you have a feeling of confidence, it is because you are drawing upon the visionary energies of the 6 and are able to see the bigger picture. True confidence comes not from knowing all the facts but trusting that what you envision with the creative energy of the 6 is truth. In the negative, confidence is attained by passing judgment and being "right," as the critical, gossipy, and pessimistic 6.

Positive: creative visionary, certainty, balanced, nurturing, peace-making, optimistic, and forward-thinking.

Negative: pessimistic, judgmental, critical, worrywart, people-pleasing, doubtful, and gossipy.

Content (1)

Meaning: "Content" vibrates to the number 1, with the isolated pioneer, new beginnings, and trailblazing energy. The 1 is the only number not divisible by any other number so it is a stand-alone energy. To be content is to draw upon the stand-alone energy of the 1. When you feel truly content, you are not striving to gain anything to become content; you are satisfied with who you are or what you have in your life, regardless of your present circumstances. It is much like the number 1, which needs nothing but itself to be content.

Positive: verbal self-expression, initiate, action, ambitious, determined, and pioneering.

Negative: aggressive, egocentric, overly driven, self-absorbed, overachieving, and single-focused.

Desire (6)

Meaning: "Desire" vibrates to the 6, the number of creativity, the nurturer, and the visionary. To desire in the positive is to utilize the creativity of the creative visionary 6 to manifest what you desire; "I have a desire to be a best-selling author and I will make it happen." In the negative, "desire" takes on a more wishful tone, making use of the pessimistic and critical 6 qualities; "I desire to find my soul mate but given my past bad luck in relationships, I'm not sure it will ever happen."

Positive: creative visionary, certainty, balanced, nurturing, peace-making, optimistic, and forward-thinking.

Negative: pessimistic, judgmental, critical, worrywart, people-pleasing, doubtful, and gossipy.

Divine (9)

Meaning: "Divine" vibrates to the 9, the ambitious, idealistic, responsible humanitarian number. The 9 is responsible for all the incredible achievements seen in the previous century; everyone born between 1889 and 1999 had at least one 9 in their date of birth. The 9 is the most active mental number, the highest change vibration, and considered the "big dreamer." Anything considered "divine" is blissful or heavenly as the idealistic big-dreamer energies of the 9 are called forth; "Meeting the queen would be simply divine!" In the negative, "divine" loses its dreamer quality, taking on a more practical and narrow-minded view as the critical and opinionated 9 takes charge; "If there is such a thing as divine intervention, now would be the time I could use some proof."

Positive: humanitarian, ambitious, responsible, justice-seeking, idealistic, and unselfish.

Negative: driven, opinionated, judgmental, critical, black and white, and narrow-minded.

Dream (5)

Meaning: "Dream" vibrates to the 5, the number of the heart, emotions, and compassionate "freedom of expression" energy. As an erratic and free-flowing energy, the 5 affords us the ability to imagine outside the box or "dream big." The positive 5 vibration acts as a window to the heart and soul of who we are, allowing us to see clearly what our spiritual self wants us to do. In the negative, we dream through the lens of the power-hungry, dominating, and bossy 5 energy.

Positive: loving, sensitive, irregular, artistic, freedom-seeking, passionate, and flexible.

Negative: uncertain, power-hungry, dominating, bossy, withdrawn, and moody.

Dynamic (6)

Meaning: "Dynamic" vibrates to the 6, the number of creativity, the nurturer, and the visionary. In creative mode with the 6 energy, "dynamic" is full of life and is motivated by the bigger picture with the creative visionary at the wheel. Those who display the trait of being dynamic often embody the optimistic and forward-thinking positive qualities of the 6; "She's such a dynamic individual, a real firecracker and so outside-the-box with her thinking." In the negative, "dynamic" acts as more of a tool or mask as the people-pleasing 6 takes the stage; "She's such a show-off in front of the boss."

Positive: creative visionary, certainty, balanced, nurturing, peace-making, optimistic, and forward-thinking

Negative: pessimistic, judgmental, critical, worrywart, people-pleasing, doubtful, and gossipy.

Easy (5)

Meaning: "Easy" vibrates to the 5, the number of the heart, emotions, and compassionate "freedom of expression" energy. As an erratic and free-flowing energy, "easy" has the freedom to bypass all obstacles; "It's easy to express my emotions when I'm free to put it into my own words." In the negative, the uncertain, withdrawn, and moody 5 comes out, giving "easy" a whiny overtone; "It's not as easy as it looks, you know."

Positive: loving, sensitive, irregular, artistic, freedom-seeking, passionate, and flexible.

Negative: uncertain, power-hungry, dominating, bossy, withdrawn, and moody.

Enjoy (6)

Meaning: "Enjoy" vibrates to the 6, the number of creativity, the nurturer, and the visionary. The 6 is a nurturing energy, direct in an outward way by nurturing others but also in an inward way by nurturing the self; "I enjoyed every moment of that experience." In the negative, "enjoy" brings forth the judgmental and critical 6; "I can't enjoy myself under these circumstances."

Positive: creative visionary, certainty, balanced, nurturing, peace-making, optimistic, and forward-thinking.

Negative: pessimistic, judgmental, critical, worrywart, people-pleasing, doubtful, and gossipy.

Essence (7)

Meaning: "Essence" vibrates to the 7, the deep, philosophical, teaching and learning number of truth-seeker energy. Working through the truth-seeker 7 vibration, use the word to get to the core or "essence" of anything; "The essence of her nature is to be harmonious." In the negative, the skeptical and distrustful 7 turns "essence" into a fact-seeker; "I'm going to get to the essence of her true motivations."

Positive: wise, contemplative, achiever, truth-seeking, determined, and hands-on.

Negative: stubborn, overactive, distrustful, hesitant, skeptical, and loner.

Essential (5)

Meaning: "Essential" vibrates to the 5, the number of the heart, emotions, and compassionate "freedom of expression" vibration. When something is essential, it is vital or fundamental. The erratic, free-flowing, freedom-seeking 5 allows you to strive for and acquire your essential piece of the puzzle in your own way without demanding it; "It's essential for me to have peace and harmony in my life to feel balanced." In the negative, the bossy 5 demands you must have an essential person, thing, or result; "It's essential that everyone be onboard with this."

Positive: loving, sensitive, irregular, artistic, freedom-seeking, passionate, and flexible.

Negative: uncertain, power-hungry, dominating, bossy, withdrawn, and moody.

Exactly (9)

Meaning: "Exactly" vibrates to the 9, the ambitious, idealistic, responsible humanitarian number. The 9 is responsible for all the incredible achievements seen in the previous century; everyone born between 1889 and 1999 had at least one 9 in their date of birth. The 9 is the most active mental number, the highest change vibration, and considered the "big dreamer." The black-and-white, right-and-wrong quality of 9 gives "exactly" its matter-of-fact and justice-seeking qualities; "Exactly! I think we're on the same page." In the negative, the judgmental, critical, and opinionated 9 passes judgment and forces its opinion; "That's not exactly what I had in mind."

Positive: humanitarian, ambitious, responsible, justice-seeking, idealistic, and unselfish.

Negative: driven, opinionated, judgmental, critical, black and white, and narrow-minded.

Exceptional (7)

Meaning: "Exceptional" vibrates to the 7, the deep, philo-sophical, teaching and learning, truth-seeker energy. You are most exceptional when you are standing in and living your own truth, which is the essence of the 7 vibration as the truth-seeker. To be "exceptional" is to be extraordi-nary, and that is only possible when we are revealing our uniqueness or truth; "That was an exceptional piano per-formance tonight; we all loved it!" In the negative, as the most active physical-plane energy, the 7 shifts from the inner to the outer, living in a state of over-activity as a means of striving to be "exceptional"; "I'm exceptional at what I do because I've worked day and night to get there."

Positive: wise, contemplative, achiever, truth-seeking, determined, and hands-on.

Negative: stubborn, overactive, distrustful, hesitant, skeptical, and loner.

Exciting (1)

Meaning: "Exciting" vibrates to the 1, with the isolated pioneer, new beginnings, and trailblazing energy. The 1 is the only number not divisible by any other number so it is a stand-alone energy. When something feels exciting, it is usually a new experience or a different take on a familiar experience. As the number of new beginnings and the pioneer, 1 is the essence of "exciting"; "It's exciting to finally be hitting the road on this adventure!" In the negative, the more physical, self-absorbed, and egocentric traits of the 1 want to create something exciting through selfishly gratifying experiences; "It's so exciting and such a rush to be center stage."

Positive: verbal self-expression, initiate, action, ambitious, determined, and pioneering.

Negative: aggressive, egocentric, overly driven, self-absorbed, overachieving, and single-focused.

Fantastic (3)

Meaning: "Fantastic" vibrates to the 3, the intellectual number of imagination, memory, and inspiration. The 3 also represents unity or coming together. "Fantastic" is a reflection of the imaginative and inspirational 3; "It is so fantastic to finally be living my dream." In the negative, the self-doubting and self-critical nature of the 3 steals the thunder from "fantastic," and it becomes something unbelievable rather than incredible; "That's a fantastic idea but it doesn't seem feasible."

Positive: analytical, intelligent, humorous, social, sensitive, observant, unity, and inspirational.

Negative: critical, vain, grandeur, self-doubting, self-critical, overanalyzing, and indecisive.

Flourish (9)

Meaning: "Flourish" vibrates to the 9, the ambitious, idealistic, responsible humanitarian number. The 9 is responsible for all the incredible achievements seen in the previous century; everyone born between 1889 and 1999 had at least one 9 in their date of birth. The 9 is the most active mental number, the highest change vibration, and considered the "big dreamer." To flourish is to grow and thrive, calling upon the ambitious big-dreamer energies of the 9; "It's important to allow your children to flourish in their own way and in their own time." In the negative, the opinionated, judgmental, and critical 9 is dominant; "She can't flourish under those conditions."

Positive: humanitarian, ambitious, responsible, justice-seeking, idealistic, and unselfish.

Negative: driven, opinionated, judgmental, critical, black and white, and narrow-minded.

Fun (5)

Meaning: "Fun" vibrates to the 5, the number of the heart, emotions, and compassionate "freedom of expression" vibration. The erratic, free-flowing, freedom-seeking, and flexible 5 is the heart and soul of "fun"; "That was so much fun! I haven't been that wild and crazy in years." In the negative, the power-hungry 5 turns "fun" into a self-gratifying, pleasure-seeking campaign; "C'mon, let's go for it. I don't care what people think, it's so much fun."

Positive: loving, sensitive, irregular, artistic, freedom-seeking, passionate, and flexible.

Negative: uncertain, power-hungry, dominating, bossy, withdrawn, and moody.

Gentle (9)

Meaning: "Gentle" vibrates to the 9, the ambitious, idealistic, responsible humanitarian number. The 9 is responsible for all the incredible achievements seen in the previous century; everyone born between 1889 and 1999 had at least one 9 in their date of birth. The 9 is the most active mental number, the highest change, and considered the "big dreamer." In the positive, the responsible and humanitarian 9 gives "gentle" its softness; "Be gentle on her, she's been hurt enough already." In the negative, the opinionated and narrow-minded 9 gives "gentle" a tougher exterior; "I'm as gentle as I can be with her given the behavior she's displayed lately."

Positive: humanitarian, ambitious, responsible, justice-seeking, idealistic, and unselfish.

Negative: driven, opinionated, judgmental, critical, black and white, and narrow-minded.

Glowing (6)

Meaning: "Glowing" vibrates to the 6, the number of creativity, the nurturer, and the visionary. "Glowing" is the embodiment of the creatively expressive visionary number 6. When you are engulfed in your own creative expression, you are glowing from the inside out; "She was glowing after her performance last night." In the negative, "glowing" is often used as more of a people-pleasing tactic; "You're glowing! Did you go to the spa?"

Positive: creative visionary, certainty, balanced, nurturing, peace-making, optimistic, and forward-thinking.

Negative: pessimistic, judgmental, critical, worrywart, people-pleasing, doubtful, and gossipy.

Grace (7)

Meaning: "Grace" vibrates to the 7, the deep, philosophical, teaching and learning, truth-seeker energy. To have or exercise grace is to capture the essence of the 7 vibration itself as the number of deeper wisdom and truth. When you express true grace, you are drawing upon your inner wisdom; it is not an expression of your personality, but rather your soul. In the negative, "grace" becomes an act or a mask representing your personality qualities. The distrustful, isolating, loner qualities of the 7 emerge, transforming "grace" from selfless soul expression to ego-based superiority, withholding mercy, charity, or forgiveness as a means of control.

Positive: wise, contemplative, achiever, truth-seeking, determined, and hands-on.

Negative: stubborn, overactive, distrustful, hesitant, skeptical, and loner.

Gratitude (6)

Meaning: "Gratitude" vibrates to the 6, the number of creativity, the nurturer, and the visionary. Having or expressing gratitude utilizes the visionary qualities of the 6. You experience gratitude for all that you have, whether good or bad and without question or judgment, as you know it is all for the greater good or bigger picture. In the negative, "gratitude" takes on a pessimistic and judgmental flavor, dipping into the negative side of the 6; "I'm grateful for this experience but…"

Positive: creative visionary, certainty, balanced, nurturing, peace-making, optimistic, and forward-thinking.

Negative: pessimistic, judgmental, critical, worrywart, people-pleasing, doubtful, and gossipy.

Great (6)

Meaning: "Great" vibrates to the 6, the number of creativity, the nurturer, and the visionary. The visionary "bigger-picture" energy of the 6 affords "great" its vast and grand energy; "It was so great to finally meet you in person!" In the negative, the pessimistic and judgmental 6 creates doubt in the impressive "great"; "She wasn't that great, I've seen better."

Positive: creative visionary, certainty, balanced, nurturing, peace-making, optimistic, and forward-thinking.

Negative: pessimistic, judgmental, critical, worrywart, people-pleasing, doubtful, and gossipy.

Grow (9)

Meaning: "Grow" vibrates to the 9, the ambitious, idealistic, responsible humanitarian number. The 9 is responsible for all the incredible achievements seen in the previous century; everyone born between 1889 and 1999 had at least one 9 in their date of birth. The 9 is the most active mental number, the highest change vibration, and considered the "big dreamer." When you grow on any level, whether mentally, emotionally, spiritually, or physically, you are changing by moving forward. In the negative, the judgmental, critical, and narrow-minded energies of the 9 take center stage, creating more obstacles to surpass in order to be able to move forward and grow; "It'll take me forever to grow out of this habit."

Positive: humanitarian, ambitious, responsible, justice-seeking, idealistic, and unselfish.

Negative: driven, opinionated, judgmental, critical, black and white, and narrow-minded.

Happy (3)

Meaning: "Happy" vibrates to the 3, the intellectual number of imagination, memory, unity, and inspiration. When you feel happy, you are living through the imaginative, inspirational, and sunny 3 energy. As the number of unity, the 3 produces a feeling of completeness, enjoyment, and satisfaction with whatever you are happy about. In the negative, that happy feeling is elusive due to the self-doubting, self-critical, and overanalyzing qualities of the 3; "I'll never be happy again."

Positive: analytical, intelligent, humorous, social, sensitive, observant, unity, and inspirational.

Negative: critical, vain, grandeur, self-doubting, self-critical, overanalyzing, and indecisive.

Harmony (4)

Meaning: "Harmony" vibrates to the 4, the solid, stable, practical, and balanced foundation number. To live in harmony is to be balanced with all things within you and without. In the positive, harmony comes from within through the balanced stability of the 4 energy; "There is nothing but harmony in my world." In the negative, harmony is sought in outer, physical, or materialistic sources; "There won't be a sense of harmony in my life until I find my soul mate."

Positive: endurance, progress, foundation, practical, balanced, organization, solid, stable, and loyal.

Negative: materialistic, impatient, addictive, instant gratification, and self-absorbed.

Healed (8)

Meaning: "Healed" vibrates to the 8, the number of wisdom, independence, confidence, and manifestation. As the most active soul-plane number, 8 has a direct link to the spiritual realm, creating a sense of wholeness and completeness. In the positive, the manifesting and doubtless powers of the 8 are tapped, creating deep and lasting healing. In the negative, an external or superficial search for sources of healing is attempted but no external avenues can produce the same depth of healing that occurs when healing takes place on the soul level.

Positive: wise, confident, assertive, independent, manifesting, assured, and loving.

Negative: detached, selfish, greedy, dominating, bossy, and attention-seeking.

Ideal (4)

Meaning: "Ideal" vibrates to the 4, the solid, stable, practical, and balanced foundation number. The hardworking and enduring positive 4 energy strives to be "ideal" in a broader sense with less focus on being the best or ideal for selfish reasons; "My ideal job would allow me to find a balance between work and family life." In the negative, "ideal" becomes perfection-seeking and materialistic, taking on the self-absorbed 4 quality; "My ideal partner would have to be into everything I enjoy or it would never work out."

Positive: endurance, progress, foundation, practical, balanced, organization, solid, stable, and loyal.

Negative: materialistic, impatient, addictive, instant gratification, and self-absorbed.

Incredible (9)

Meaning: "Incredible" vibrates to the 9, the ambitious, idealistic, responsible humanitarian number. The 9 is responsible for all the incredible achievements seen in the previous century; everyone born between 1889 and 1999 had at least one 9 in their date of birth. The 9 is the most active mental number, the highest change vibration, and considered the "big dreamer." "Incredible" relies on the big-dreamer 9 energy to take it over the top into extraordinary territory; "That's incredible! You finished it in record time." In the negative, the judging, opinionated, and critical 9 deflates "incredible"; "Sounds incredible, but hardly believable."

Positive: humanitarian, ambitious, responsible, justice-seeking, idealistic, and unselfish.

Negative: driven, opinionated, judgmental, critical, black and white, and narrow-minded.

Inspire (9)

Meaning: "Inspire" vibrates to the 9, the ambitious, idealistic, responsible humanitarian number. The 9 is responsible for all the incredible achievements seen in the previous century; everyone born between 1889 and 1999 had at least one 9 in their date of birth. The 9 is the most active mental number, the highest change vibration, and considered the "big dreamer." When you inspire someone, you infuse them with the positive qualities of the 9—the idealistic, ambitious, big-dreamer energy. In the negative, you aim to inspire others by sharing your opinion of what you think they should be or do.

Positive: humanitarian, ambitious, responsible, justice-seeking, idealistic, and unselfish.

Negative: driven, opinionated, judgmental, critical, black and white, and narrow-minded.

Invigorating (1)

Meaning: "Invigorating" vibrates to the number 1, with the isolated pioneer, new beginnings, and trailblazing energy. The 1 is the only number not divisible by any other number so it is a stand-alone energy. As the number of new beginnings and trailblazer energy, "invigorating" is alive with stimulating energy; "Taking the scenic route home is always so interesting and invigorating. We should do it more often." In the negative, the aggressive, egocentric, and overly driven 1 says for something to feel invigorating, it has to strive to be bigger and better; "It's invigorating to always surpass my sales goal each week."

Positive: verbal self-expression, initiate, action, ambitious, determined, and pioneering.

Negative: aggressive, egocentric, overly driven, self-absorbed, overachieving, and single-focused.

Invincible (9)

Meaning: "Invincible" vibrates to the 9, the ambitious, idealistic, responsible humanitarian number. The 9 is responsible for all the incredible achievements seen in the previous century; everyone born between 1889 and 1999 had at least one 9 in their date of birth. The 9 is the most active mental number, the highest change vibration, and considered the "big dreamer." The ambitious, determined, and idealistic 9 gives "invincible" its unshakable determination to conquer. In the positive, the humanitarian 9 takes ego out of the equation, the desire to be invincible reserved for broader goals and visions; "When it comes to my charity work and winning a marathon to raise money, I'm invincible." In the negative, the judging and criticizing 9 knocks the pegs out from under "invincible"; "She seems invincible now, but her days are numbered in that sport."

Positive: humanitarian, ambitious, responsible, justice-seeking, idealistic, and unselfish.

Negative: driven, opinionated, judgmental, critical, black and white, and narrow-minded.

Kind (2)

Meaning: "Kind" vibrates to the 2, the number of intuition, sensitivity, cooperation, and dualistic energy. As the gentle, sensitive, peaceful, harmonious, and cooperative 2, to be kind is to be the essence of the 2 in its purest form; "She is such a kind and thoughtful person." In the negative, the whiny and passive codependent 2 makes "kind" appear clingy and needy rather than generously supportive; "He's always been so kind to him but never to me. I don't know what I did wrong."

Positive: balance, cooperation, sensitive, intuitive, supportive, and harmonious.

Negative: contrast, codependent, uncertain, submissive, passive, and hypersensitive.

Joy (5)

Meaning: "Joy" vibrates to the 5, the number of the heart, emotions, and compassionate "freedom of expression" energy. "Joy" is a higher state of happiness, full of freedom, passion, and flexibility to express your emotions without hindrance. In the positive, "joy" is the epitome of all the 5 energy holds. In the negative, the dominating, uncertain, and withdrawn qualities of the 5 prevent the uninhibited expression of "joy" and its true nature.

Positive: loving, sensitive, irregular, artistic, freedom-seeking, passionate, and flexible.

Negative: uncertain, power-hungry, dominating, bossy, withdrawn, and moody.

Live (3)

Meaning: "Live" vibrates to the 3, the intellectual number of imagination, memory, and inspiration. The 3 also represents unity or coming together. As the inspirational and imaginative number, when you truly live, you are living an inspired life imagined by you; "Live like there's no tomorrow." In the negative, your ability to live becomes inhibited by the self-doubting, critical, and indecisive energy of the 3; "When will I ever get to live my life the way I want to?"

Positive: analytical, intelligent, humorous, social, sensitive, observant, unity, and inspirational.

Negative: critical, vain, grandeur, self-doubting, self-critical, overanalyzing, and indecisive.

Love (9)

Meaning: "Love" vibrates to the 9, the ambitious, idealistic, responsible humanitarian number. The 9 is responsible for all the incredible achievements seen in the previous century; everyone born between 1889 and 1999 had at least one 9 in their date of birth. The 9 is the most active mental number, the highest change vibration, and considered the "big dreamer." It also represents the beginning and end of a cycle and, in some cultures, the 9 is referred to as the complete number. In the case of "love," the 9 brings truth to the saying, "love is all there is." In the positive, "love" is unconditional, selfless, humanitarian energy. In the negative, judgmental and critical opinions place conditions on "love."

Positive: humanitarian, ambitious, responsible, justice-seeking, idealistic, and unselfish.

Negative: driven, opinionated, judgmental, critical, black and white, and narrow-minded.

Magic (6)

Meaning: "Magic" vibrates to the 6, the number of creativity, the nurturer, and the visionary. To experience "magic" is to see beyond the possible or the known, drawing from the creative visionary energies of the 6 to see beyond and create your own magic in life; "Being here was pure magic. So surreal!" In the negative, the pessimistic 6 is front and center; "It's going to take a whole lot of magic to get us out of this one."

Positive: creative visionary, certainty, balanced, nurturing, peace-making, optimistic, and forward-thinking.

Negative: pessimistic, judgmental, critical, worrywart, people-pleasing, doubtful, and gossipy.

Miracle (7)

Meaning: "Miracle" vibrates to the 7, the deep, philosophical, teaching and learning, truth-seeker energy. A miracle occurs from a place deeper than the physical. As the truth-seeker number 7, "miracle" harnesses deep, philosophical truth-seeker energy; "It's a miracle beyond explanation." In the negative, the distrustful and skeptical 7 needs more fact than faith to prove the validity of a miracle; "It appeared to be a miracle that happened overnight, but it was really a product of all her accumulated efforts."

Positive: wise, contemplative, achiever, truth-seeking, determined, and hands-on.

Negative: stubborn, overactive, distrustful, hesitant, skeptical, and loner.

Natural (6)

Meaning: "Natural" vibrates to the 6, the number of creativity, the nurturer, and the visionary. To be "natural" is to effortlessly be who you are. Working through the visionary 6 energy, when you can see the bigger picture, it's easy to be natural and not feel the need to pretend to be something or someone you're not for the sake of pleasing others, as being natural means you know who you are and what you have to offer; "She's a natural at this." In the negative, the people-pleasing and critical 6 puts a damper on your ability to be natural; "Just act natural and they'll never know the difference."

Positive: creative visionary, certainty, balanced, nurturing, peace-making, optimistic, and forward-thinking.

Negative: pessimistic, judgmental, critical, worrywart, people-pleasing, doubtful, and gossipy.

New (6)

Meaning: "New" vibrates to the 6, the number of creativity, the nurturer, and the visionary. To create something new is to utilize the creative visionary energy of the 6; "I've got a brand-new idea to present that I know you'll love." In the negative, the pessimistic and critical 6 energy resists anything new; "I don't know about this new fad, seems a little crazy to me."

Positive: creative visionary, certainty, balanced, nurturing, peace-making, optimistic, and forward-thinking.

Negative: pessimistic, judgmental, critical, worrywart, people-pleasing, doubtful, and gossipy.

Now (7)

Meaning: "Now" vibrates to the 7, the deep, philosophical, teaching and learning, truth-seeker energy. When you "live in the now," you are not concerned with the past or future. Living in the now is the essence of the 7 vibration as the number of deeper wisdom and truth. The regrets of the past and worries of the future are not a concern to the soul and you do not have a desire to know or understand the past or future while centered in the now. In the negative, "now" pulls from the skeptical and stubborn qualities of the 7, creating a demanding scenario of attempting to control the outcome or the "how" of whatever you are focusing on in the present moment.

Positive: wise, contemplative, achiever, truth-seeking, determined, and hands-on.

Negative: stubborn, overactive, distrustful, hesitant, skeptical, and loner.

Open (5)

Meaning: "Open" vibrates to the 5, the number of the heart, emotions, and compassionate "freedom of expression" energy. To be open is to express through the freedom-seeking, irregular, flexible, and sensitive energies of the 5; "I'm open to the possibilities." In the negative, "open" takes on the vibration of dominating and being power-hungry, seeking to be "open" as a means of accumulating more "power" on either a mental, emotional, or physical level; "I'm open to it if it's worth my time."

Positive: loving, sensitive, irregular, artistic, freedom-seeking, passionate, and flexible.

Negative: uncertain, power-hungry, dominating, bossy, withdrawn, and moody.

Outstanding (9)

Meaning: "Outstanding" vibrates to the 9, the ambitious, idealistic, responsible humanitarian number. The 9 is responsible for all the incredible achievements seen in the previous century; everyone born between 1889 and 1999 had at least one 9 in their date of birth. The 9 is the most active mental number, the highest change vibration, and considered the "big dreamer." To be outstanding is to draw up the ambitious, idealistic, and big-dreamer energy of the 9, stepping outside your comfort zone as the pioneer. In the negative, the high expectations and critical, opinionated views of the 9 turn "outstanding" into a nearly unreachable goal, both for you and others you may be judging as "outstanding."

Positive: Humanitarian, ambitious, responsible, justice-seeking, idealistic, unselfish.

Negative: Driven, opinionated, judgmental, critical, black and white, narrow-minded.

Passion (3)

Meaning: "Passion" vibrates to the 3, the intellectual number of imagination, memory, and inspiration. The 3 also represents unity or coming together. When you experience passion for a new idea, you feel inspired and imaginative along with a sense of unity or a "coming together" of your concept. "Passion" in the positive conveys that inspiration and imagination are limitless. In the negative, "passion" takes on the limiting qualities of the 3 with a self-criticizing, overanalyzing, and critical outlook, placing reservations on your passion.

Positive: analytical, intelligent, humorous, social, sensitive, observant, unity, and inspirational.

Negative: critical, vain, grandeur, self-doubting, self-critical, overanalyzing, and indecisive.

Perfect (1)

Meaning: "Perfect" vibrates to the number 1, with the isolated pioneer, new beginnings, and trailblazing energy. The 1 is the only number not divisible by any other number so it is a stand-alone energy. The number 1 is perfect on its own, not needing any other numbers or vibrations to be complete. "Perfect" represents the stand-alone energy of the 1; "You're perfect just the way you are." In the negative, the overly driven and egocentric 1 strives to become perfect, seeking to add or subtract through achievement; "My weight isn't quite perfect for my height yet—I've got to shave off a few more pounds."

Positive: verbal self-expression, initiate, action, ambitious, determined, and pioneering.

Negative: aggressive, egocentric, overly driven, self-absorbed, overachieving, and single-focused.

Positive (7)

Meaning: "Positive" vibrates to the 7, the deep, philosophical, teaching and learning, truth-seeker energy. The truth-seeking 7 is always striving as the achiever to find the deeper meaning in all things and it is "positive" it will find it; "I'm positive we're on the right path, let's keep going." In the negative, that certainty is painted with distrust, hesitancy, and skepticism; "Are you positive this is what you want?"

Positive: wise, contemplative, achiever, truth-seeking, determined, and hands-on.

Negative: stubborn, overactive, distrustful, hesitant, skeptical, and loner.

Possibility (2)

Meaning: "Possibility" vibrates to the 2, the number of intuition, sensitivity, cooperation, and dualistic energy. When you embrace possibility, you are centered in the cooperative, harmonious, intuitive side of the 2, as well as its dualistic nature with two separate or opposing sides. In the positive, "possibility" expresses intuitive trust; "I'm open to the possibility." In the negative, you resist or oppose possibility by stepping into the codependent, uncertain, and contrasting side of the 2, which reveals a hint of doubt; "It's a possibility."

Positive: balance, cooperation, sensitive, intuitive, supportive, and harmonious.

Negative: contrast, codependent, uncertain, submissive, passive, and hypersensitive.

Prosper (8)

Meaning: "Prosper" vibrates to the 8, the number of wisdom, independence, confidence, and manifestation. As the most active soul-plane number, 8 has a direct link to the spiritual realm, creating a sense of wholeness and completeness. Manifesting with the wise, confident, and assertive 8 energy, you can truly prosper on all levels; "I prosper even in times of recession because I'm always confident in my financial decisions." In the negative, "prosper" puts on a selfish mask, seeking to thrive by leveraging or dominating others; "It's difficult to prosper in this role when you're surrounded by idiots."

Positive: wise, confident, assertive, independent, manifesting, assured, and loving.

Negative: detached, selfish, greedy, dominating, bossy, and attention-seeking.

Proud (2)

Meaning: "Proud" vibrates to the 2, the number of intuition, sensitivity, cooperation, and dualistic energy. The cooperative, supportive, and intuitive 2 allows you to feel proud, not only of yourself but of others, and does not seek acknowledgment; "I'm so proud of you!" In the negative, the codependent and hypersensitive 2 seeks out acknowledgement from others as a means to feel good; "Aren't you proud of me?"

Positive: balance, cooperation, sensitive, intuitive, supportive, and harmonious.

Negative: contrast, codependent, uncertain, submissive, passive, and hypersensitive.

Pure (6)

Meaning: "Pure" vibrates to the 6, the number of creativity, the nurturer, and the visionary. The positive 6 sees beyond any flaws with its creative visionary energy; "I know that deep down he's pure of heart." In the negative, "pure" is a moral issue and encourages people-pleasing; "Girls should remain pure until at least the age of sixteen."

Positive: creative visionary, certainty, balanced, nurturing, peace-making, optimistic, and forward-thinking.

Negative: pessimistic, judgmental, critical, worrywart, people-pleasing, doubtful, and gossipy.

Refreshing (1)

Meaning: "Refreshing" vibrates to the number 1, with the isolated pioneer, new beginnings, and trailblazing energy. The 1 is the only number not divisible by any other number so it is a stand-alone energy. As the number of new beginnings, the 1 is "refreshing." The uniqueness and individuality of the stand-alone 1 makes anyone or anything become a refreshing change of pace; "It's so refreshing to get away from all the chaos of everyday life." In the negative, "refreshing" is sought after through physical gratification as the overly driven, egocentric, and aggressive 1 takes the reins; "It's refreshing to date different people regularly, as it keeps life exciting. I don't plan on settling down anytime soon."

Positive: verbal self-expression, initiate, action, ambitious, determined, and pioneering.

Negative: aggressive, egocentric, overly driven, self-absorbed, overachieving, and single-focused.

Satisfaction (1)

Meaning: "Satisfaction" vibrates to the number 1, with the isolated pioneer, new beginnings, and trailblazing energy. The 1 is the only number not divisible by any other number so it is a stand-alone energy. To be in a state of satisfaction is to feel content with what is now. The 1 is content with itself as it is and needs nothing else to feel a sense of satisfaction; "I'm feeling such satisfaction with my life as I get older." In the negative, the egocentric and overachieving energies of the 1 push to the outer limits to achieve satisfaction; "I won't have a sense of satisfaction with my work until I achieve the Noble Peace Prize."

Positive: verbal self-expression, initiate, action, ambitious, determined, and pioneering.

Negative: aggressive, egocentric, overly driven, self-absorbed, overachieving, and single-focused.

Sensational (3)

Meaning: "Sensational" vibrates to the 3, the intellectual number of imagination, memory, and inspiration. The 3 also represents unity or coming together. To be sensational is to be amazing or astounding, thanks to the imaginative, inspirational, and positive 3 energy; "You were sensational, a true star in the making." In the negative, the vain, grandiose side of the 3 turns "sensational" into needing to be the center of attention and being overly concerned with the views of others; "I've just got to be sensational tonight and knock their socks off or I'll be the laughingstock of the team."

Positive: analytical, intelligent, humorous, social, sensitive, observant, unity, and inspirational.

Negative: critical, vain, grandeur, self-doubting, self-critical, overanalyzing, and indecisive.

Serene (3)

Meaning: "Serene" vibrates to the 3, the intellectual number of imagination, memory, and inspiration. The 3 also represents unity or coming together. As the number of unity, when things come together, it creates a serene and tranquil energy where you are at peace because everything has come together as it should be; "It is so serene just sitting here with you under the stars." In the negative, the self-doubting and critical 3 never truly allows a feeling of being serene to manifest; "The serene moments in this house are nonexistent!"

Positive: analytical, intelligent, humorous, social, sensitive, observant, unity, and inspirational.

Negative: critical, vain, grandeur, self-doubting, self-critical, overanalyzing, and indecisive.

Strong (3)

Meaning: "Strong" vibrates to the 3, the intellectual number of imagination, memory, and inspiration. The 3 also represents unity or coming together. Living through the inspirational and unified positive 3 energy, it's easy to be strong and solid; "I consider myself a strong woman because I'm confident in who I am." In the negative, the self-doubting and self-critical 3 questions how strong you really are or can be; "I'm not as strong as I thought I could be in this rocky relationship."

Positive: analytical, intelligent, humorous, social, sensitive, observant, unity, and inspirational.

Negative: critical, vain, grandeur, self-doubting, self-critical, overanalyzing, and indecisive.

Success (8)

Meaning: "Success" vibrates to the 8, the number of wisdom, independence, confidence, and manifestation. As the most active soul-plane number, 8 has a direct link to the spiritual realm, creating a sense of wholeness and completeness. A sense of accomplishment or success in the positive comes from the wise and confident soulful knowing of the 8. Success is a personal victory, and not for attention-seeking reasons; "Success came for me late in the game, but it doesn't matter; what truly matters is that I enjoyed the whole journey to get here." In the negative, the 8 flaunts success as a showy display tainted with selfishness; "I'm the only person in my family to achieve this level of success and fortune."

Positive: wise, confident, assertive, independent, manifesting, assured, and loving.

Negative: detached, selfish, greedy, dominating, bossy, and attention-seeking.

Superb (9)

Meaning: "Superb" vibrates to the 9, the ambitious, idealistic, responsible humanitarian number. The 9 is responsible for all the incredible achievements seen in the previous century; everyone born between 1889 and 1999 had at least one 9 in their date of birth. The 9 is the most active mental number, the highest change vibration, and considered the "big dreamer." The idealistic outlook of the positive 9 gives "superb" its outstanding shine factor; "That meal was superb—the best I've ever had." In the negative, "superb" is tainted with judgmental and critical nitpicking; "It was a superb performance, but the lead singer had a bit of a crackle to his voice."

Positive: humanitarian, ambitious, responsible, justice-seeking, idealistic, and unselfish.

Negative: driven, opinionated, judgmental, critical, black and white, and narrow-minded.

Sure (9)

Meaning: "Sure" vibrates to the 9, the ambitious, idealistic, responsible humanitarian number. The 9 is responsible for all the incredible achievements seen in the previous century; everyone born between 1889 and 1999 had at least one 9 in their date of birth. The 9 is the most active mental number, the highest change vibration, and considered the "big dreamer"; 9 is also considered the number of completion, as it represents both the beginning and the end of a cycle. To be sure is to feel complete, displaying the idealistic energy of the 9 in the positive; "Sure thing." In the negative, "sure" has an underlying tone of the judgmental, critical, and opinionated 9; "Are you sure that's a good idea?"

Positive: humanitarian, ambitious, responsible, justice-seeking, idealistic, and unselfish.

Negative: driven, opinionated, judgmental, critical, black and white, and narrow-minded.

Terrific (7)

Meaning: "Terrific" vibrates to the 7, the deep, philosophical, teaching and learning, truth-seeker energy. In the positive, the feeling of being terrific shines from within, matching the vibration of the wise and truth-filled 7 energy. In the negative, "terrific" has an underlying tone of distrust and skepticism, used more as a mask to hide your true emotions. "I'm terrific" is a phrase that could be utilized in both the positive and negative, yet mean completely different things depending on the vibration behind it.

Positive: wise, contemplative, achiever, truth-seeking, determined, and hands-on.

Negative: stubborn, overactive, distrustful, hesitant, skeptical, and loner.

Thrive (1)

Meaning: "Thrive" vibrates to the number 1, with the isolated pioneer, new beginnings, and trailblazing energy. The 1 is the only number not divisible by any other number so it is a stand-alone energy. To thrive is to grow and change beyond what you are now. A flower that grows to blossom does not strive to be more than it is but rather seeks to flourish or thrive to be what it was meant to be, nothing more or less. In the negative, "thrive" represents the egocentric and overachieving energies of the 1, pushing to increase or accumulate excess as a means to thrive.

Positive: verbal self-expression, initiate, action, ambitious, determined, and pioneering.

Negative: aggressive, egocentric, overly driven, self-absorbed, overachieving, and single-focused.

Tingle (4)

Meaning: "Tingle" vibrates to the 4, the solid, stable, practical, and balanced foundation number. As a very solid, stable, and physical-based energy, the 4 gives "tingle" its link to the physical. Although a tingle may or may not be initiated from a physical source, "tingle" is almost always associated with a physical sensation yet felt on a soulful level as well; "I felt a tingle all through my body the first time we kissed." In the negative, "tingle" is associated more with addictive sensation-seeking and instant gratification in the physical sense; "I love the tingle I get from a hot stone massage."

Positive: endurance, progress, foundation, practical, balanced, organization, solid, stable, and loyal.

Negative: materialistic, impatient, addictive, instant gratification, and self-absorbed.

Totally (6)

Meaning: "Totally" vibrates to the 6, the number of creativity, the nurturer, and the visionary. Working through the visionary "bigger picture" energy of the 6, "totally" is firm and absolute in its vibration. In the negative, "totally" takes on the underlying tone of the people-pleasing 6. Instead of a feeling of absolution, there is doubt and pessimism and "totally" is spoken as a means to appear that you are in complete agreement.

Positive: creative visionary, certainty, balanced, nurturing, peace-making, optimistic, and forward-thinking.

Negative: pessimistic, judgmental, critical, worrywart, people-pleasing, doubtful, and gossipy.

Transformation (3)

Meaning: "Transformation" vibrates to the 3, the intellectual number of imagination, memory, and inspiration. The 3 also represents unity or coming together. As the inspirational and imaginative number, the 3 change of "transformation" comes from imagining and feeling inspired that you can be or do anything. You can create a transformation from a positive or a negative standpoint in any area of your life, depending on whether you focus on the inspirational and imaginative qualities of the 3 or the self-doubting, self-critical, and indecisive ones.

Positive: analytical, intelligent, humorous, social, sensitive, observant, unity, and inspirational.

Negative: critical, vain, grandeur, self-doubting, self-critical, overanalyzing, and indecisive.

True (1)

Meaning: "True" vibrates to the number 1, with the isolated pioneer, new beginnings, and trailblazing energy. The 1 is the only number not divisible by any other number so it is a stand-alone energy. When something is true, there is no doubt, as the number 1 is the absolute number. As a complete number, 1 does not need to add or subtract anything or prove itself in any way that it is whole as it is. In the negative, the aggressive, egocentric, and overachieving traits of the 1 are highlighted as a means to prove that something or someone is true.

Positive: verbal self-expression, initiate, action, ambitious, determined, and pioneering.

Negative: aggressive, egocentric, overly driven, self-absorbed, overachieving, and single-focused.

Trust (8)

Meaning: "Trust" vibrates to the 8, the number of wisdom, independence, confidence, and manifestation. As the most active soul-plane number, 8 has a direct link to the spiritual realm, creating a sense of wholeness and completeness. Another word for "trust" is "faith," which comes from a deeper sense of trust within and is not based solely on outer facts or information. When you trust, you pull upon the confident and assured characteristics of the 8 as a direct link to your soulful energy; "I trust you." In the negative, "trust" is based more on the selfish side of the 8 and desiring outer information or proof that someone or something is worthy of your trust; "I can't trust you after what you did to me."

Positive: wise, confident, assertive, independent, manifesting, assured, and loving.

Negative: detached, selfish, greedy, dominating, bossy, and attention-seeking.

Truth (6)

Meaning: "Truth" vibrates to the 6, the number of creativity, the nurturer, and the visionary. When you know the truth, it is because you can see the bigger picture through the visionary energy of the 6. In the positive, the truth is not doubted, as you are able to see how it fits into the broader picture; "It is the absolute truth." In the negative, there is an undertone of pessimism, doubt, and criticism of the truth; "Tell me the truth!"

Positive: creative visionary, certainty, balanced, nurturing, peace-making, optimistic, and forward-thinking.

Negative: pessimistic, judgmental, critical, worrywart, people-pleasing, doubtful, and gossipy.

Ultimate (8)

Meaning: "Ultimate" vibrates to the 8, the number of wisdom, independence, confidence, and manifestation. As the most active soul-plane number, 8 has a direct link to the spiritual realm, creating a sense of wholeness and completeness. To have an ultimate experience is to possess an inner knowing that is fundamental in some way. In the negative, "ultimate" seeks to be flashy or showy in order to prove outwardly that it is an important or "ultimate" experience.

Positive: wise, confident, assertive, independent, manifesting, assured, and loving.

Negative: detached, selfish, greedy, dominating, bossy, and attention-seeking.

Undeniably (8)

Meaning: "Undeniably" vibrates to the 8, the number of wisdom, independence, confidence, and manifestation. As the most active soul-plane number, 8 has a direct link to the spiritual realm, creating a sense of wholeness and completeness. The 8 energy is doubtless in the positive. "Undeniably" is also doubtless because it is the 8 vibration, the number of confidence and wisdom; "You are undeniably correct, no doubt about it." In the negative, "undeniably" favors the 8 qualities of selfishness, domination, and attention-seeking, looking to always be right and fighting to prove it; "You know I'm undeniably right and I can prove it."

Positive: wise, confident, assertive, independent, manifesting, assured, and loving.

Negative: detached, selfish, greedy, dominating, bossy, and attention-seeking.

Unique (6)

Meaning: "Unique" vibrates to the 6, the number of creativity, the nurturer, and the visionary. When you look beyond face value, utilizing the visionary 6 energy in the positive, you can see the unique qualities in all and appreciate them as part of the whole picture; "She's unique and her actions are very admirable." In the negative, "unique" is more about standing out and playing the people-pleaser; "My talents in this industry are unique; you won't find a better salesman."

Positive: creative visionary, certainty, balanced, nurturing, peace-making, optimistic, and forward-thinking.

Negative: pessimistic, judgmental, critical, worrywart, people-pleasing, doubtful, and gossipy.

Unsurpassed (4)

Meaning: "Unsurpassed" vibrates to the 4, the solid, stable, practical, and balanced foundation number. The enduring, solid, stable, and loyal 4 wins the race and gives "unsurpassed" the energy to go the distance, earning an A for effort; "The level of customer service at that hotel is unsurpassed in the industry." In the negative, it is all about acquiring an unsurpassed achievement level for materialistic and self-absorbed reasons; "Thanks to the tweaks I had done to my car recently, it's unsurpassed on the track."

Positive: endurance, progress, foundation, practical, balanced, organization, solid, stable, and loyal.

Negative: materialistic, impatient, addictive, instant gratification, and self-absorbed.

Valuable (4)

Meaning: "Valuable" vibrates to the 4, the solid, stable, practical, and balanced foundation number. Something is valuable when it adds to your life's foundation in some way. In the positive, the things that you consider to be most valuable are the pieces of your life's foundation that are priceless and intangible (memory, life lessons, etc.). In the negative, the adding of something valuable to your foundation is focused on gaining from a more physical or materialistic viewpoint.

Positive: endurance, progress, foundation, practical, balanced, organization, solid, stable, and loyal.

Negative: materialistic, impatient, addictive, instant gratification, and self-absorbed.

Vibrant (5)

Meaning: "Vibrant" vibrates to the 5, the number of the heart, emotions, and compassionate "freedom of expression" energy. When you feel vibrant, you are alive with the "freedom of expression" energy of the number 5. In the positive, there is no agenda, just the sensation of vitality in your own energy. In the negative, "vibrant" seeks to dazzle or shine more brilliantly than someone or something else, stepping into the dominating and power-hungry side of the 5 vibration; "I feel so vibrant today" or "I'm as vibrant at fifty as most twenty-somethings are."

Positive: loving, sensitive, irregular, artistic, freedom-seeking, passionate, and flexible.

Negative: uncertain, power-hungry, dominating, bossy, withdrawn, and moody.

Whole (9)

Meaning: "Whole" vibrates to the 9, the ambitious, idealistic, responsible humanitarian number. The 9 is responsible for all the incredible achievements seen in the previous century; everyone born between 1889 and 1999 had at least one 9 in their date of birth. The 9 is the most active mental number, the highest change vibration, and considered the "big dreamer." To be whole is to have all pieces of the "pie" present and intact. In the positive, the 9 energy is unselfish and humanitarian, facilitating a view of yourself as whole regardless of your present state or circumstances; "We all have flaws, but I am whole and complete as I am now." In the negative, your view of the whole vision of yourself is faced with the judging and critical opinions of the 9 vibration; "I'll feel whole and complete when I lose these last 5 pounds."

Positive: humanitarian, ambitious, responsible, justice-seeking, idealistic, and unselfish.

Negative: driven, opinionated, judgmental, critical, black and white, and narrow-minded.

Winner (2)

Meaning: "Winner" vibrates to the 2, the number of intuition, sensitivity, cooperation, and dualistic energy. In the positive, the cooperative, supportive, and sensitive 2 qualities state that we are all winners, regardless of who or what we are. In the negative, the dualistic nature of the 2 stands front and center, stating that there is no gray area when it comes to being a winner—you either are or you aren't. The 2 in the negative highlights its hypersensitive and passive nature, causing you to compare your flaws to those you perceive to be more of a winner than you.

Positive: balance, cooperation, sensitive, intuitive, supportive, and harmonious.

Negative: contrast, codependent, uncertain, submissive, passive, and hypersensitive.

Wise (2)

Meaning: "Wise" vibrates to the 2, the number of intuition, sensitivity, cooperation, and dualistic energy. In the positive, "wise" draws from the wellspring of intuition and sensitivity of the 2; "You can already tell, even at this age, that she's wise beyond her years." In the negative, the 2 is displayed as seemingly separate and uncertain, detaching from the intuitive voice within. Instead of a strong sense of knowing, "wise" defends itself as the hypersensitive 2; "Listen kid, you may be smart but I'm wise."

Positive: balance, cooperation, sensitive, intuitive, supportive, and harmonious.

Negative: contrast, codependent, uncertain, submissive, passive, and hypersensitive.

Wonderful (1)

Meaning: "Wonderful" vibrates to the number 1, with the isolated pioneer, new beginnings, and trailblazing energy. The 1 is the only number not divisible by any other number so it is a stand-alone energy. For something to be wonderful, it has to better than the norm. With the pioneering 1 in the positive, "wonderful" is sure to rise above the average; "What a wonderful surprise! I've never experienced that before." In the negative, "wonderful" seeks to be in the spotlight with the egocentric and overachieving 1; "I think I did a wonderful job if I do say so myself."

Positive: **verbal self-expression, initiate, action, ambitious, determined, and pioneering.**

Negative: **aggressive, egocentric, overly driven, self-absorbed, overachieving, and single-focused.**

Wow (7)

Meaning: "Wow" vibrates to the 7, the deep, philosophical, teaching and learning, truth-seeker energy. As the truth-seeker, the 7 brings the "wow" factor. When you apply "wow" to anything, it is an awe-filled vibration because you are in amazement at some piece of new knowledge or experience; "Wow, I never knew that about her." In the negative, instead of amazement and wonder, "wow" has an undertone of the distrustful and skeptical 1; "Wow, there had better be a good reason for this attitude, missy."

Positive: **wise, contemplative, achiever, truth-seeking, determined, and hands-on.**

Negative: **stubborn, overactive, distrustful, hesitant, skeptical, and loner.**

Yes (4)

Meaning: "Yes" vibrates to the 4, the solid, stable, practical, and balanced foundation number. When you say yes to something and mean it, you are drawing from the solid, practical, and balanced foundation energy of the 4. Your "yes" is grounded firmly in reality. In the negative, "yes" takes on the impatient and instant-gratification energies of the 4, creating an impulsive "yes" lacking certainty; "I'll say yes to anything fun!"

Positive: endurance, progress, foundation, practical, balanced, organization, solid, stable, and loyal.

Negative: materialistic, impatient, addictive, instant gratification, and self-absorbed.

Zest (7)

Meaning: "Zest" vibrates to the 7, the deep, philosophical, teaching and learning, truth-seeker energy. As the most active physical-plane number, in the positive the 7 takes you on a search for truth by living life through personal experience. The relentless searcher, the 7 energy has a "zest" for life; "I've got a newfound zest for life now that I'm back to creating my artwork." In the negative, the feeling of "zest" is sought out more for materialistic and physically gratifying reasons rather than experiencing life for the personal truths it reveals; "I've got more zest in my step when my pocket is full of money and I'm headed out for a night on the town."

Positive: wise, contemplative, achiever, truth-seeking, determined, and hands-on.

Negative: stubborn, overactive, distrustful, hesitant, skeptical, and loner.

Top Negative Words

Afraid (3)

Meaning: "Afraid" vibrates to the 3, the intellectual number of imagination, memory, and inspiration. The 3 also represents unity or coming together. In the negative, "afraid" feeds completely off the self-doubting, self-critical energies of the 3; "I'm afraid I'll never find true love." In the positive, the imaginative and inspirational energies of the 3 vibration lift the fears associated with being afraid; "I'm not afraid of a challenge, I welcome it!"

Positive: analytical, intelligent, humorous, social, sensitive, observant, unity, and inspirational.

Negative: critical, vain, grandeur, self-doubting, self-critical, overanalyzing, and indecisive.

Alone (2)

Meaning: "Alone" vibrates to the 2, the number of intuition, sensitivity, cooperation, and dualistic energy. In the negative, the dualistic, opposing or separated energy of the 2 gives "alone" its isolated feeling. When divided, 2 creates a double 1, the isolated stand-alone number; "I'm all alone in this world." In the positive, "alone" relies on the supportive and cooperative 2 traits shifting the feelings of isolation to a sense of being supported even when alone; "I can do this alone."

Positive: balance, cooperation, sensitive, intuitive, supportive, and harmonious.

Negative: contrast, codependent, uncertain, submissive, passive, and hypersensitive.

Angry (2)

Meaning: "Angry" vibrates to the 2, the number of intuition, sensitivity, cooperation, and dualistic energy. In the negative, the intuitive and sensitive side of the 2 is clouded and you are unable to clearly see the reasons behind what has caused you to be angry; "Don't even talk to me; I'm so angry with you right now." In the positive, "angry" loses its steam quickly, softened by the cooperative, harmonious, and intuitive 2; "I can't stay angry at you; I know you didn't mean it."

Positive: balance, cooperation, sensitive, intuitive, supportive, and harmonious.

Negative: contrast, codependent, uncertain, submissive, passive, and hypersensitive.

Anguish (7)

Meaning: "Anguish" vibrates to the 7, the deep, philosophical, teaching and learning, truth-seeker energy. As the most active physical-plane number, 7 in the negative seeks to suffer alone with its distrustful, stubborn, and hesitant qualities; "I'm going through such anguish over this breakup and I don't have anyone to turn to who understands." In the positive, the 7 is determined to uncover the reasons behind such anguish; "I'll help her get to the bottom of her anguish. She deserves to be happy."

Positive: wise, contemplative, achiever, truth-seeking, determined, and hands-on.

Negative: stubborn, overactive, distrustful, hesitant, skeptical, and loner.

Ashamed (6)

Meaning: "Ashamed" vibrates to the 6, the number of creativity, the nurturer, and the visionary. In the negative, "ashamed" is focused on the people-pleasing qualities of the 6; "I'm so ashamed of what I said; I'll never be able to show my face in this town again." In the positive, "ashamed" is able to see the bigger picture as the visionary 6, softening the devastating blow; "I'm not ashamed of my actions because I know it was the right thing to say at the time."

Positive: creative visionary, certainty, balanced, nurturing, peace-making, optimistic, and forward-thinking.

Negative: pessimistic, judgmental, critical, worrywart, people-pleasing, doubtful, and gossipy.

Avoid (6)

Meaning: "Avoid" vibrates to the 6, the number of creativity, the nurturer, and the visionary. Steering clear of judgment and criticism, "avoid" is concerned with what other people might think as the negative 6 energy; "I know I can't avoid them forever, but I can sure try." In the positive, the visionary 6 can see that to avoid is to stall and hinder a necessary resolution for the benefit of the broader picture; "I'm just beating around the bush, I can't avoid her anymore."

Positive: creative visionary, certainty, balanced, nurturing, peace-making, optimistic, and forward-thinking.

Negative: pessimistic, judgmental, critical, worrywart, people-pleasing, doubtful, and gossipy.

Awful (9)

Meaning: "Awful" vibrates to the 9, the ambitious, idealistic, responsible humanitarian number. The 9 is responsible for all the incredible achievements seen in the previous century; everyone born between 1889 and 1999 had at least one 9 in their date of birth. The 9 is the most active mental number, the highest change vibration, and considered the "big dreamer." In the negative, "awful" is critical, judgmental, and opinionated without knowing any or all of the facts; "Isn't it awful what she said to him?" In the positive, "awful" is ambitious, idealistic, and humanitarian; "I'm sure it isn't that awful, I think I'll try it."

Positive: humanitarian, ambitious, responsible, justice-seeking, idealistic, and unselfish.

Negative: driven, opinionated, judgmental, critical, black and white, and narrow-minded.

Awkward (9)

Meaning: "Awkward" vibrates to the 9, the ambitious, idealistic, responsible humanitarian number. The 9 is responsible for all the incredible achievements seen in the previous century; everyone born between 1889 and 1999 had at least one 9 in their date of birth. The 9 is the most active mental number, the highest change vibration, and considered the "big dreamer." In the negative, the black-and-white, right-and-wrong, perfectionist, critical 9 contributes to the uncomfortable feeling of "awkward." When you feel awkward, you are self-conscious of your perceived imperfections; "That was so awkward! I felt so out of place with that elite group of women." In the positive, the humanitarian side of the 9 strives to rectify "awkward," softening its perfectionist view; "There's no need to feel awkward, we're all family."

Positive: humanitarian, ambitious, responsible, justice-seeking, idealistic, and unselfish.

Negative: driven, opinionated, judgmental, critical, black and white, and narrow-minded.

Bad (7)

Meaning: "Bad" vibrates to the 7, the deep, philosophical, teaching and learning, truth-seeker energy. In the negative, the 7 vibration carries a deep sense of distrust of the self and others, not based on any outer facts or information; "I just know something bad is going to happen." In the positive, pulling from the deeper truth-seeking energy that is the 7 in its true form, "bad" benefits from the deep sense of inner trust that comes from tapping into your truth; "I'm sure it won't be as bad as it seems."

Positive: wise, contemplative, achiever, truth-seeking, determined, and hands-on.

Negative: stubborn, overactive, distrustful, hesitant, skeptical, and loner.

Beaten (2)

Meaning: "Beaten" vibrates to the 2, the number of intuition, sensitivity, cooperation, and dualistic energy. In the negative, the dualistic, opposing, separated energy of the 2 gives "beaten" its defeated undertone; "I was beaten at the marathon." In the positive, "beaten" relies on the supportive and cooperative 2 traits shifting the feelings of defeat to a sense of being supported and not alone, even when faced with potential defeat or loss; "I will not be beaten down or subdued."

Positive: balance, cooperation, sensitive, intuitive, supportive, and harmonious.

Negative: contrast, codependent, uncertain, submissive, passive, and hypersensitive.

Belittle (4)

Meaning: "Belittle" vibrates to the 4, the solid, stable, practical, and balanced foundation number. In the negative, you belittle someone from a materialistic or physical and self-absorbed standpoint, focusing on what you have that they don't; "My boss would always belittle me in front of his manager to make himself look good." In the positive, a more practical and balanced view is taken, based on the positive qualities of the 4; "That was unacceptable to belittle her in front of her friends."

Positive: endurance, progress, foundation, practical, balanced, organization, solid, stable, and loyal.

Negative: materialistic, impatient, addictive, instant gratification, and self-absorbed.

Betray (8)

Meaning: "Betray" vibrates to the 8, the number of wisdom, independence, confidence, and manifestation. As the most active soul-plane number, 8 has a direct link to the spiritual realm, creating a sense of wholeness and completeness. To betray is to deceive or be disloyal; living through the negative qualities of the 8, "betray" becomes detached, selfish, and greedy; "If you betray me, you'll pay for it." In the positive, the wise and assured energies take over, creating a deeper view of "betray"; "I'm sure there's a good reason for her to betray me in this way, considering she's always been honest with me in the past."

Positive: wise, confident, assertive, independent, manifesting, assured, and loving.

Negative: detached, selfish, greedy, dominating, bossy, and attention-seeking.

Bitter (2)

Meaning: "Bitter" vibrates to the 2, the number of intuition, sensitivity, cooperation, and dualistic energy. In the negative, the dualistic, opposing, separated energy of the 2 gives "bitter" its detached and divided stance; "She's bitter about the breakup because he cheated on her." In the positive, "bitter" translates into a softened outlook from the cooperative and harmonious 2 energy; "I'm not bitter because I know she meant well."

Positive: balance, cooperation, sensitive, intuitive, supportive, and harmonious.

Negative: contrast, codependent, uncertain, submissive, passive, and hypersensitive.

Blame (6)

Meaning: "Blame" vibrates to the 6, the number of creativity, the nurturer, and the visionary. In the negative, "blame" judges and is critical and pessimistic; "He's to blame, I just know it." In the positive, the visionary and nurturing sides of the 6 come forth and instead of pointing fingers, leaves the door open for the bigger picture to be viewed; "No one is really to blame here."

Positive: creative visionary, certainty, balanced, nurturing, peace-making, optimistic, and forward-thinking.

Negative: pessimistic, judgmental, critical, worrywart, people-pleasing, doubtful, and gossipy.

Burden (1)

Meaning: "Burden" vibrates to the 1, the isolated pioneer, new beginnings, and trailblazing energy. The 1 is the only number not divisible by any other number, making it is a stand-alone energy. As an isolated number, 1 in the negative believes "burden" is something to bear alone, playing the victim; "He's such a burden but there's no one else to take care of him but me." In the positive, the overly driven, egocentric, and aggressive 1 views a burden as something to overcome or discard if it becomes too inhibiting; "She's a burden to my company and I'm going to have to cut her loose."

Positive: verbal self-expression, initiate, action, ambitious, determined, and pioneering.

Negative: aggressive, egocentric, overly driven, self-absorbed, overachieving, and single-focused.

But (7)

Meaning: "But" vibrates to the 7, the deep, philosophical, teaching and learning, truth-seeker energy. In the negative, "but" is used to express distrust of the self or others when you are not centered in your truth; "I wanted to join in but I was afraid they wouldn't like me." In the positive, when trust is incorporated into "but," it displays a knowing or truth from within; "I didn't have the same level of credentials as the other candidates, but it didn't matter, I knew I was worthy of that award."

Positive: wise, contemplative, achiever, truth-seeking, determined, and hands-on.

Negative: stubborn, overactive, distrustful, hesitant, skeptical, and loner.

Can't (2)

Meaning: "Can't" vibrates to the 2, the number of intuition, sensitivity, cooperation, and dualistic energy. In the negative, the dualistic, opposing, or separated energy of the 2 gives "can't" its uncertain, codependent, and passive tone; "I can't do this!" In the positive, "can't" leans toward the balanced, intuitive, and supportive traits of the 2; "They say I can't do this, but I'm sure going to try."

Positive: balance, cooperation, sensitive, intuitive, supportive, and harmonious.

Negative: contrast, codependent, uncertain, submissive, passive, and hypersensitive.

Challenge (4)

Meaning: "Challenge" vibrates to the 4, the solid, stable, practical, and balanced foundation number. In the negative, the impatient and instant gratification-seeking 4 gives rise to losing steam quickly when it comes to taking on a challenge; "I'm not sure I can weather this challenge." As the physical energy considered the number of the "doer," in the positive sense, "challenge" is all about doing in the physical sense and putting one's nose to the grindstone to get the job done; "I'm up for the challenge."

Positive: endurance, progress, foundation, practical, balanced, organization, solid, stable, and loyal.

Negative: materialistic, impatient, addictive, instant gratification, and self-absorbed.

Cheated (1)

Meaning: "Cheated" vibrates to the number 1, with the isolated pioneer, new beginnings, and trailblazing energy. The 1 is the only number not divisible by any other number so it is a stand-alone energy. Appearing as the separated loner, the negative 1 takes being cheated personally and seeks revenge or rectification; "She cheated me out of a chance at the top position in the company and I can't let her get away with that." In the positive, the 1 seeks to overcome being cheated through its qualities of ambition, determination, and action; "She cheated me out of the opportunity to speak at that event, but there will be other events and other opportunities."

Positive: verbal self-expression, initiate, action, ambitious, determined, and pioneering.

Negative: aggressive, egocentric, overly driven, self-absorbed, overachieving, and single-focused.

Chaotic (5)

Meaning: "Chaotic" vibrates to the 5, the number of the heart, emotions, and compassionate "freedom of expression" energy. In the negative, "chaotic" is exhibiting the uncertain and erratic 5 energy that is moody and unpredictable; "My life is so chaotic right now and it's very stressful to cope with." In the positive, the freedom-seeking and flexible 5 thrives on chaotic situations; "My life is chaotic, but I like it that way. It keeps things interesting."

Positive: loving, sensitive, irregular, artistic, freedom-seeking, passionate, and flexible.

Negative: uncertain, power-hungry, dominating, bossy, withdrawn, and moody.

Clingy (7)

Meaning: "Clingy" vibrates to the 7, the deep, philosophical, teaching and learning, truth-seeker energy. In the negative, the distrustful and skeptical 7 causes "clingy" to be needy and demanding from a lack of trust; "I know I've been clingy lately, but I'm a little gun-shy after my last relationship." In the positive, "clingy" becomes a challenge for the truth-seeking 7 to get to the bottom of; "Why are you so clingy lately? Let's talk about this."

Positive: wise, contemplative, achiever, truth-seeking, determined, and hands-on.

Negative: stubborn, overactive, distrustful, hesitant, skeptical, and loner.

Closed (4)

Meaning: "Closed" vibrates to the 4, the solid, stable, practical, and balanced foundation number. In the negative, the impatient and instant gratification-seeking 4 loses steam for the challenge when it hits anything that is closed; "No matter how hard I try, I keep coming up against closed doors." As the physical energy considered the number of the "doer," when something is closed, whether it be a relationship, opportunity, or path, the enduring, stable, positive 4 aims to find balance; "This may seem like a closed door for now, but I'm determined to make it work."

Positive: endurance, progress, foundation, practical, balanced, organization, solid, stable, and loyal.

Negative: materialistic, impatient, addictive, instant gratification, and self-absorbed.

Codependent (6)

Meaning: "Codependent" vibrates to the 6, the number of creativity, the nurturer, and the visionary. In the negative, when the visionary 6 loses sight of the bigger picture, becoming codependent is a natural response, needing to be guided by outside sources instead of its own inner vision; "He's become so codependent in this new relationship. It's sad that such an outgoing guy has lost sight of his individuality." In the positive, the creative visionary 6 sees the broader scope of why a temporary codependent state might benefit the whole; "She's just codependent now because she's in a new environment. We'll soon see the old her back full force."

Positive: creative visionary, certainty, balanced, nurturing, peace-making, optimistic, and forward-thinking.

Negative: Pessimistic, judgmental, critical, worrywart, people-pleasing, doubtful, and gossipy.

Competitive (2)

Meaning: "Competitive" vibrates to the 2, the number of intuition, sensitivity, cooperation, and dualistic energy. In the negative, the dualistic, opposing, or separated energy of the 2 gives "competitive" its fighting gloves; "He's so competitive with everyone and everything. Someone needs to tell him it's not all about winning." In the positive, "competitive" turns friendlier with the sensitive and cooperative 2 energy; "I love a little friendly competitive action, especially when it's all in good fun."

Positive: balance, cooperation, sensitive, intuitive, supportive, and harmonious.

Negative: contrast, codependent, uncertain, submissive, passive, and hypersensitive.

Concern (9)

Meaning: "Concern" vibrates to the 9, the ambitious, idealistic, responsible humanitarian number. The 9 is responsible for all the incredible achievements seen in the previous century; everyone born between 1889 and 1999 had at least one 9 in their date of birth. The 9 is the most active mental number, the highest change vibration, and considered the "big dreamer." In the negative, "concern" takes on a critical and judgmental stance through the idealistic 9 energy; "I'm concerned she won't be an asset to the team." In the positive, the humanitarian qualities come forth to express genuine and selfless concern without judgment or criticism; "I'm concerned for your health working all those hours."

Positive: humanitarian, ambitious, responsible, justice-seeking, idealistic, and unselfish.

Negative: driven, opinionated, judgmental, critical, black and white, and narrow-minded.

Confined (7)

Meaning: "Confined" vibrates to the 7, the deep, philosophical, teaching and learning, truth-seeker energy. To feel confined is to have a sense of entrapment, imprisonment, or being shut up in some way. In the negative, "confined" exhibits symptoms of distrust; "This relationship feels so trapping and confined." In the positive, the deeper sense of inner trust associated the positive 7 energy is able to see past the confining situation with a knowing it is for a greater purpose than just your restriction; "My life seems restricted and I feel confined by work at the moment, but I know if I work hard, I'll get where I want to be." Gandhi is a perfect example of someone who viewed restricting and confining situations in the positive.

Positive: wise, contemplative, achiever, truth-seeking, determined, and hands-on.

Negative: stubborn, overactive, distrustful, hesitant, skeptical, and loner.

Consumed (4)

Meaning: "Consumed" vibrates to the 4, the solid, stable, practical, and balanced foundation number. In the negative, the impatient and instant gratification-seeking 4 loses steam and feels swamped or consumed with the circumstances; "This term paper has consumed my life for the past month. I didn't realize how much work it would be." In the positive, the hardworking, enduring, and foundation-building 4 is consumed with its work and loving it; "I'm happiest when I'm consumed with a new project."

Positive: endurance, progress, foundation, practical, balanced, organization, solid, stable, and loyal.

Negative: materialistic, impatient, addictive, instant gratification, and self-absorbed.

Cold (7)

Meaning: "Cold" vibrates to the 7, the deep, philosophical, teaching and learning, truth-seeker energy. In the negative, "cold" draws upon the isolated and distrustful qualities of the 7, making it distant and difficult to reach; "You've been so cold lately. Is there something you want to tell me?" In the positive, the deep-thinking and truth-seeking 7 can also create a detached scenario with "cold"; "Whenever he's hard at work on a writing project, he seems detached and cold but that's just him in creative mode."

Positive: wise, contemplative, achiever, truth-seeking, determined, and hands-on.

Negative: stubborn, overactive, distrustful, hesitant, skeptical, and loner.

Conflicted (8)

Meaning: "Conflicted" vibrates to the 8, the number of wisdom, independence, confidence, and manifestation. As the most active soul-plane number, 8 has a direct link to the spiritual realm, creating a sense of wholeness and completeness. In the negative, "conflicted" pulls out the detached 8 energy; "I'm conflicted with this choice but I'm the only one that can make it." In the positive, "conflicted" utilizes the wise and loving qualities of the 8; "I'm conflicted about who to team up with because I don't want to step on any toes, but I know I have to decide what's best for all involved."

Positive: wise, confident, assertive, independent, manifesting, assured, and loving.

Negative: detached, selfish, greedy, dominating, bossy, and attention-seeking.

Confused (6)

Meaning: "Confused" vibrates to the 6, the number of creativity, the nurturer, and the visionary. In the negative, when the visionary 6 loses sight of the bigger picture, it becomes confused; "I'm not sure what the right thing is. I'm so confused!" In the positive, the creative visionary 6 sees the bigger picture of why being confused may be necessary in the short term; "I know you're confused now, but when you get older, you'll understand why she had to leave."

Positive: creative visionary, certainty, balanced, nurturing, peace-making, optimistic, and forward-thinking.

Negative: pessimistic, judgmental, critical, worrywart, people-pleasing, doubtful, and gossipy.

Control (7)

Meaning: "Control vibrates to the 7, the deep, philosophical, teaching and learning, truth-seeker energy. In the negative, the stubborn, distrustful, and skeptical 7 seeks to control what it doesn't understand or trust completely; "She's such a control freak. Someone should tell her to loosen up." In the positive, the truth-seeking and achieving 7 takes charge in order to shed some light on the truth; "Don't worry guys, I've got it all under control, we'll be fine."

Positive: wise, contemplative, achiever, truth-seeking, determined, and hands-on.

Negative: stubborn, overactive, distrustful, hesitant, skeptical, and loner.

Couldn't (1)

Meaning: "Couldn't" vibrates to the number 1, with the isolated pioneer, new beginnings, and trailblazing energy. The 1 is the only number not divisible by any other number so it is a stand-alone energy. In the negative, "couldn't" is lacking the pioneering and trailblazing qualities of the 1 and instead focuses on the self-absorbed, self-centered, and isolating energy; "I couldn't do it because I had no one to help me." In the positive, the trailblazing pioneer energy steps forward; "They said I couldn't do it, but I showed them."

Positive: verbal self-expression, initiate, action, ambitious, determined, and pioneering.

Negative: aggressive, egocentric, overly driven, self-absorbed, overachieving, and single-focused.

Critical (3)

Meaning: "Critical" vibrates to the 3, the intellectual number of imagination, memory, and inspiration. The 3 also represents unity or coming together. In the negative, "critical" is the epitome of the self-doubting and self-critical 3 energy; "You're so incredibly critical, no matter what I do. I give up!" In the positive, "critical" is softened by the inspirational and imaginative 3; "She seems critical and negative but I've seen her softer side peek through a few times."

Positive: analytical, intelligent, humorous, social, sensitive, observant, unity, and inspirational.

Negative: critical, vain, grandeur, self-doubting, self-critical, overanalyzing, and indecisive.

Criticize (3)

Meaning: "Criticize" vibrates to the 3, the intellectual number of imagination, memory, and inspiration. The 3 also represents unity or coming together. In the negative, "criticize" gets its harshness from the self-doubting and self-critical 3 energy; "You always criticize her for doing the wrong thing but never praise her for the right things." In the positive, "criticize" is subdued by the inspirational and imaginative 3; "She tends to criticize me, but I take it with a grain of salt and let it roll off my back."

Positive: analytical, intelligent, humorous, social, sensitive, observant, unity, and inspirational.

Negative: critical, vain, grandeur, self-doubting, self-critical, overanalyzing, and indecisive.

Damaged (8)

Meaning: "Damaged" vibrates to the 8, the number of wisdom, independence, confidence, and manifestation. As the most active soul-plane number, 8 has a direct link to the spiritual realm, creating a sense of wholeness and completeness. In the negative, the 8 energy is detached, cold, and selfish, giving "damaged" an air of being imperfect or not worthy; "She's damaged goods, not worth my time." The 8 in the positive is the number of wisdom, independence, and loving by nature. It does not view anyone or anything as damaged or tainted, but rather sees the deeper wisdom of what has happened and why; "Everyone thinks my past abuse has damaged me beyond repair, but I know who I truly am."

Positive: wise, confident, assertive, independent, manifesting, assured, and loving.

Negative: detached, selfish, greedy, dominating, bossy, and attention-seeking.

Defeated (5)

Meaning: "Defeated" vibrates to the 5, the number of the heart, emotions, and compassionate "freedom of expression" energy. In the negative, the uncertain, withdrawn and moody 5 takes center stage, creating the feeling of being defeated; "I've been defeated at my own game. I'm done for now." In the positive, the freedom-seeking, passionate, and flexible 5 turns "defeated" into a reason to bust free and create again; "I may be defeated at this stage but there's nothing stopping me from trying other avenues."

Positive: loving, sensitive, irregular, artistic, freedom-seeking, passionate, and flexible.

Negative: uncertain, power-hungry, dominating, bossy, withdrawn, and moody.

Deficient (3)

Meaning: "Deficient" vibrates to the 3, the intellectual number of imagination, memory, and inspiration. The 3 also represents unity or coming together. In the negative, the self-doubting, self-critical, and overanalyzing 3 manifests being deficient in anything and everything; "I was always deficient in confidence, a painfully shy child." In the positive, the inspirational and unity-driven 3 wants anything deficient to be corrected and balanced; "Even though I'm deficient in a sense of direction, I always get to where I'm going eventually!"

Positive: analytical, intelligent, humorous, social, sensitive, observant, unity, and inspirational.

Negative: critical, vain, grandeur, self-doubting, self-critical, overanalyzing, and indecisive.

Demand (5)

Meaning: "Demand" vibrates to the 5, the number of the heart, emotions, and compassionate "freedom of expression" energy. In the negative, the power-hungry, dominating, and bossy 5 will make a demand to exert power or control; "I demand you treat me with respect." In the positive, the freedom-seeking and passionate 5 may demand and be assertive for the purpose of protecting freedom but does so in a loving and sensitive way; "The only thing I demand in this relationship is space to do the things I love."

Positive: loving, sensitive, irregular, artistic, freedom-seeking, passionate, and flexible.

Negative: uncertain, power-hungry, dominating, bossy, withdrawn, and moody.

Depressed (5)

Meaning: "Depressed" vibrates to the 5, the number of the heart, emotions, and compassionate "freedom of expression" energy. The negative 5 is moody and withdrawn, which is the essence of "depressed"; "I'm so depressed right now, I can't believe I'm stuck in a situation I swore I'd never be." In the positive, the loving, sensitive, and freedom-seeking 5 strives to avoid or eliminate ruts like the state of depression as it is a freedom-squashing energy; "I can't let this experience keep me depressed and miserable. It's just not my nature to be this way."

Positive: loving, sensitive, irregular, artistic, freedom-seeking, passionate, and flexible.

Negative: uncertain, power-hungry, dominating, bossy, withdrawn, and moody.

Deserve (6)

Meaning: "Deserve" vibrates to the 6, the number of creativity, the nurturer, and the visionary. In the negative, "deserve" is about whether or not you are worthy of something, relying on the critical, pessimistic, and judgmental qualities of the 6; "You don't deserve my respect with that behavior." In the positive, "deserve" takes a broader approach, focusing on the optimistic and forward-thinking energy of the 6 in the positive; "If you're willing to put in the effort, you deserve the recognition."

Positive: creative visionary, certainty, balanced, nurturing, peace-making, optimistic, and forward-thinking.

Negative: pessimistic, judgmental, critical, worrywart, people-pleasing, doubtful, and gossipy.

Despair (9)

Meaning: "Despair" vibrates to the 9, the ambitious, idealistic, responsible humanitarian number. The 9 is responsible for all the incredible achievements seen in the previous century; everyone born between 1889 and 1999 had at least one 9 in their date of birth. The critical, right-and-wrong outlook of the negative 9 is quick to bask in misery and despair if things don't go as envisioned, playing the role of victim; "The breakup was so unexpected. I'm in such a state of despair over it." In the positive, the unselfish humanitarian aims to pick up despair and put a smile on its face; "Don't despair. Things are looking brighter every day."

Positive: humanitarian, ambitious, responsible, justice-seeking, idealistic, and unselfish.

Negative: driven, opinionated, judgmental, critical, black and white, and narrow-minded.

Destructive (2)

Meaning: "Destructive" vibrates to the 2, the number of intuition, sensitivity, cooperation, and dualistic energy. In the negative, 2 is an unpredictable and destructive force as the contrasting, uncertain, and hypersensitive energy; "She gets incredibly self-destructive when he's not around. He's become her crutch." In the positive, the balanced, cooperative, sensitive, and harmony-seeking 2 wants to cure any destructive energy; "Please put some thought into what you say to her. She's very fragile and your comments are destructive."

Positive: balance, cooperation, sensitive, intuitive, supportive, and harmonious.

Negative: contrast, codependent, uncertain, submissive, passive, and hypersensitive.

Detest (1)

Meaning: "Detest" vibrates to the number 1, with the isolated pioneer, new beginnings, and trailblazing energy. The 1 is the only number not divisible by any other number so it is a stand-alone energy. In the negative, the aggressive, egocentric, and overachieving 1 outlook is to detest anything that doesn't align with its self-focused morals and beliefs; "I detest stupidity in any form." In the positive, "detest" is less applied for the purpose of judging others and used more for personal motivation factors. However, it is one of those words that can still carry a hint of negativity, even in the positive; "I detest myself when I let my diet slip. I'm not myself, even with just a few extra pounds."

Positive: verbal self-expression, initiate, action, ambitious, determined, and pioneering.

Negative: aggressive, egocentric, overly driven, self-absorbed, overachieving, and single-focused.

Difficult (9)

Meaning: "Difficult" vibrates to the 9, the ambitious, idealistic, responsible humanitarian number. The 9 is responsible for all the incredible achievements seen in the previous century; everyone born between 1889 and 1999 had at least one 9 in their date of birth. Something is difficult to the opinionated, judgmental, and narrow-minded negative 9 when a person, place, or situation does not match the rigid ideals of the 9; "He makes a mountain out of a molehill and is always so difficult to deal with." In the positive, the softer humanitarian energy shines through using the big-dreamer energy in a more loving way; "She's not as difficult as she seems; cut her some slack."

Positive: humanitarian, ambitious, responsible, justice-seeking, idealistic, and unselfish.

Negative: driven, opinionated, judgmental, critical, black and white, and narrow-minded.

Disappointed (6)

Meaning: "Disappointed" vibrates to the 6, the number of creativity, the nurturer, and the visionary. In the negative, "disappointed" is a reflection of the doubting and people-pleasing 6; "She's disappointed in me, I know it." In the positive, the visionary steps forward to shine a light on the bigger picture; "I'm not disappointed in you, because I know you tried your best and that's all that really matters."

Positive: creative visionary, certainty, balanced, nurturing, peace-making, optimistic, and forward-thinking.

Negative: pessimistic, judgmental, critical, worrywart, people-pleasing, doubtful, and gossipy.

Directionless (8)

Meaning: "Directionless" vibrates to the 8, the number of wisdom, independence, confidence, and manifestation. As the most active soul-plane number, 8 has a direct link to the spiritual realm, creating a sense of wholeness and completeness. In the negative the 8 is out of alignment with its truest nature as the wise and confident number. A feeling of being directionless occurs when we are cut off from that deeper wisdom within; "After I lost my job last month, I've been feeling so directionless. I'm not sure what my next chapter is." In the positive, the wise and assured 8 breathes hope into "directionless"; "At the moment, I'm directionless, but I know something is just around the corner for me, I can feel it."

Positive: wise, confident, assertive, independent, manifesting, assured, and loving.

Negative: detached, selfish, greedy, dominating, bossy, and attention-seeking.

Discontent (4)

Meaning: "Discontent" vibrates to the 4, the solid, stable, practical, and balanced foundation number. The impatient and restless 4 in the negative causes discontent without the stamina to solve it; "I'm so discontent in my life, but I don't know where to begin to change it. I'm overwhelmed." In the positive, the progressive, enduring, and practical 4 uses the discontentment as fuel to keep moving forward; "Whenever I'm feeling discontent in any way, I know it's time to take action on some level."

Positive: endurance, progress, foundation, practical, balanced, organization, solid, stable, and loyal.

Negative: materialistic, impatient, addictive, instant gratification, and self-absorbed.

Doubt (2)

Meaning: "Doubt" vibrates to the 2, the number of intuition, sensitivity, cooperation, and dualistic energy. In the negative, the dualistic, opposing, or separated energy of the 2 casts doubt on a person or situation; "I seriously doubt she's going to win the race." In the positive, the separate and opposing energies are replaced by a viewpoint based on intuition, sensitivity, and cooperation; "I never doubted you, not even for a moment."

Positive: balance, cooperation, sensitive, intuitive, supportive, and harmonious.

Negative: contrast, codependent, uncertain, submissive, passive, and hypersensitive.

Down (2)

Meaning: "Down" vibrates to the 2, the number of intuition, sensitivity, cooperation, and dualistic energy. The uncertain, codependent, and hypersensitive 2 doesn't have to look far for something to bring it down; "I feel so down when you're not near me. You're my drug." In the positive, the balanced, sensitive, supportive, and cooperative 2 makes an effort to find a harmonious resolution; "I know you're feeling down now but wait until you get the call. It will be good news."

Positive: balance, cooperation, sensitive, intuitive, supportive, and harmonious.

Negative: contrast, codependent, uncertain, submissive, passive, and hypersensitive.

Drained (1)

Meaning: "Drained" vibrates to the number 1, with the isolated pioneer, new beginnings, and trailblazing energy. The 1 is the only number not divisible by any other number so it is a stand-alone energy. When the 1 is in the negative form, it lacks its ambitious, determined, and pioneering qualities. "Drained" channels a lack of these very qualities; "I'm so drained lately. I don't know how to get my energy back." In the positive, the initiating, action-seeking, and ambitious 1 vibration is motivated to overcome any symptoms of being drained; "I'm usually drained after a group meeting but I've learned that a little quiet time fixes me right up again."

Positive: verbal self-expression, initiate, action, ambitious, determined, and pioneering.

Negative: aggressive, egocentric, overly driven, self-absorbed, overachieving, and single-focused.

Dread (5)

Meaning: "Dread" vibrates to the 5, the number of the heart, emotions, and compassionate "freedom of expression" energy. When the 5 is in a negative space, it brings forth the qualities of uncertainty, moodiness, being withdrawn, and avoidance. These are reflected in the word "dread"; "I dread the first day of school tomorrow with this terrible haircut." The positive, flexible, and freedom-seeking 5 not only doesn't feel dread to the same degree as the negative 5, there may even be a sense of excitement about conquering the unknown; "I'm nervous and dread meeting with the acting scouts, but I'm fairly confident I can ace the performance."

Positive: loving, sensitive, irregular, artistic, freedom-seeking, passionate, and flexible.

Negative: uncertain, power-hungry, dominating, bossy, withdrawn, and moody.

Elusive (3)

Meaning: "Elusive" vibrates to the 3, the intellectual number of imagination, memory, and inspiration. The 3 also represents unity or coming together. In the negative, the 3 is wishy-washy due to its self-doubt, self-criticism, and indecisive traits. Many things become elusive to the negative 3 due to the outlook it holds; "True happiness has always been elusive because I'm so self-conscious." In the positive, the intelligent, imaginative, and inspirational 3 is curious about that which appears to be elusive; "I've always had a fascination for the mysterious and elusive things in life. Makes life exciting and an adventure!"

Positive: analytical, intelligent, humorous, social, sensitive, observant, unity, and inspirational.

Negative: critical, vain, grandeur, self-doubting, self-critical, overanalyzing, and indecisive.

Empty (7)

Meaning: "Empty" vibrates to the 7, the deep, philosophical, teaching and learning, truth-seeker energy. In the negative, the 7 is distrustful, hesitant, and skeptical, often feeling emptiness if its fragile sense of trust is broken; "My heart feels empty inside after the way he left." In the positive, the 7 is forever the truth-seeker, wanting to reveal the deeper meaning in all things; "I need to uncover why I'm still feeling so empty inside, despite the great promotion I just received."

Positive: wise, contemplative, achiever, truth-seeking, determined, and hands-on.

Negative: stubborn, overactive, distrustful, hesitant, skeptical, and loner.

Excessive (3)

Meaning: "Excessive" vibrates to the 3, the intellectual number of imagination, memory, and inspiration. The 3 also represents unity or coming together. The negative 3 is very familiar with being excessive and is frequently guilty of over-the-top self-doubt and self-criticism as well as being overly critical of others; "That's a bit excessive, don't you think? There's a time and a place for such inappropriate behavior, and it's not here." The positive 3 is also known for being excessive in terms of imaginative and inspirational energy. The 3 is often called the bipolar number due to its extreme positive and negative sides; "I know my enthusiasm can be a bit excessive, but I get so excited when it comes to new ideas."

Positive: analytical, intelligent, humorous, social, sensitive, observant, unity, and inspirational.

Negative: critical, vain, grandeur, self-doubting, self-critical, overanalyzing, and indecisive.

Fear (3)

Meaning: "Fear" vibrates to the 3, the intellectual number of imagination, memory, and inspiration. The 3 also represents unity or coming together. In the negative, "fear" is based in the self-doubting, self-critical, and indecisive energies of the 3; "I fear I'll lose everything if I take that chance." In the positive, the inspirational and imaginative energies of the positive 3 come flooding back in, giving fear less power over you; "I have a fear of spiders but I'm willing to do what it takes to overcome it."

Positive: analytical, intelligent, humorous, social, sensitive, observant, unity, and inspirational.

Negative: critical, vain, grandeur, self-doubting, self-critical, overanalyzing, and indecisive.

Flaw (6)

Meaning: "Flaw" vibrates to the 6, the number of creativity, the nurturer, and the visionary. In the negative, the critical and judgmental 6 points out the flaw like the elephant in the room; "It's a great plan, but I see just one minor flaw with the strategy." In the positive, the peace-making, visionary energy of the 6 shows you the bigger picture and that there are no mistakes or flaws, only choices; "You may see a flaw but I think you're perfect and just as you should be."

Positive: creative visionary, certainty, balanced, nurturing, peace-making, optimistic, and forward-thinking.

Negative: pessimistic, judgmental, critical, worrywart, people-pleasing, doubtful, and gossipy.

Force (2)

Meaning: "Force" vibrates to the 2, the number of intuition, sensitivity, cooperation, and dualistic energy. In the negative, the dualistic, opposing, or separated energy of the 2 makes "force" a dueling power struggle; "I'll have to use all my willpower and force to kick this habit." In the positive, "force" becomes a harmonious, cooperative, and supportive energy, embracing the positive qualities of the 2 vibration; "Together we're a force to be reckoned with."

Positive: balance, cooperation, sensitive, intuitive, supportive, and harmonious.

Negative: contrast, codependent, uncertain, submissive, passive, and hypersensitive.

Frustration (8)

Meaning: "Frustration" vibrates to the 8, the number of wisdom, independence, confidence, and manifestation. As the most active soul-plane number, 8 has a direct link to the spiritual realm, creating a sense of wholeness and completeness. As the independent number, the negative 8 tends to suffer from episodes of frustration, especially in situations where it is smothered or apprehended; "She causes me such frustration when she won't hear me out." In the positive, the wise and assured 8 understands that whatever is causing the feeling of frustration is either temporary or for a deeper purpose; "There's frustration at the office now but things will smooth out once the new employees settle in."

Positive: wise, confident, assertive, independent, manifesting, assured, and loving.

Negative: detached, selfish, greedy, dominating, bossy, and attention-seeking.

Grief (9)

Meaning: "Grief" vibrates to the 9, the ambitious, idealistic, responsible humanitarian number. The 9 is responsible for all the incredible achievements seen in the previous century; everyone born between 1889 and 1999 had at least one 9 in their date of birth. The 9 is the most active mental number, the highest change vibration, and considered the "big dreamer." In the negative, "grief" is miserable and full of anguish from the self-imposed idealistic limitations set by viewing the situation through the narrow-minded, black-and-white, negative 9 vibration; "He gave her grief for not having it done to his specifications." In the positive, the softener and less judgmental humanitarian 9 comes through, changing the misery of the negative grief into a hopeful scenario that will pass soon; "I'm feeling grief now, but I know it's just temporary as a part of loss."

Positive: humanitarian, ambitious, responsible, justice-seeking, idealistic, and unselfish.

Negative: driven, opinionated, judgmental, critical, black and white, and narrow-minded.

Guilt (6)

Meaning: "Guilt" vibrates to the 6, the number of creativity, the nurturer, and the visionary. In the negative, "guilt" plays the blame game, focused on passing judgment and being critical of actions of the individual or others; "I carry a sense of guilt from not telling her how I really felt before she died." In the positive, you are able to see past the guilt and view the bigger picture through the visionary energy of the 6; "I'm releasing my feelings of guilt about this situation because I know it really didn't have anything to do with my actions."

Positive: creative visionary, certainty, balanced, nurturing, peace-making, optimistic, and forward-thinking.

Negative: pessimistic, judgmental, critical, worrywart, people-pleasing, doubtful, and gossipy.

Hard (4)

Meaning: "Hard" vibrates to the 4, the solid, stable, practical, and balanced foundation number. In the negative, "hard" embodies the impatient and self-absorbed energy of the 4, creating an obstacle when there really isn't one; "It's just too hard, I can't do it!" In the positive, the enduring, progressive, and stable energies of the 4 transform "hard" into something that is tough but not unbreakable; "This course is hard work, but nothing I can't handle."

Positive: endurance, progress, foundation, practical, balanced, organization, solid, stable, and loyal.

Negative: materialistic, impatient, addictive, instant gratification, and self-absorbed.

Hassle (1)

Meaning: "Hassle" vibrates to the number 1, with the isolated pioneer, new beginnings, and trailblazing energy. The 1 is the only number not divisible by any other number so it is a stand-alone energy. "Hassle" in the negative wears the self-absorbed and single-focused 1 energy; "It's too much of a hassle for me to be bothered with their nonsense." In the positive, to the pioneering, determined, and ambitious 1, nothing is too much of a hassle; "As much as it's a hassle, I know it's a part of the plan and needs to be done to get there."

Positive: verbal self-expression, initiate, action, ambitious, determined, and pioneering.

Negative: aggressive, egocentric, overly driven, self-absorbed, overachieving, and single-focused.

Hate (7)

Meaning: "Hate" vibrates to the 7, the deep, philosophical, teaching and learning, truth-seeker energy. In the negative, when you think, speak, or write "hate," it is comparable to being energetically stripped bare. It is a volatile inner-change vibration, revealing much truth about the object of "hate"; "I hate you!" In the positive, "hate" is softened as it is able to draw from the deeper wisdom and truth of the 7; "I've come to realize I don't hate her; it's just her behavior that's challenging at times."

Positive: wise, contemplative, achiever, truth-seeking, determined, and hands-on.

Negative: stubborn, overactive, distrustful, hesitant, skeptical, and loner.

Helpless (6)

Meaning: "Helpless" vibrates to the 6, the number of creativity, the nurturer, and the visionary. In the negative, "helpless" is working through the people-pleasing and pessimistic energy of the 6. When you feel helpless, you feel powerless to make a change. Being the people-pleasing pessimist, it is easy to feel helpless because you are not able to see the bigger picture; "I feel so helpless to change this relationship but I don't want to hurt him." In the positive, "helpless" is seen in a wider view through the lens of the visionary 6 vibration; "There's no need to feel helpless in this situation; you have all the help you need to move forward."

Positive: creative visionary, certainty, balanced, nurturing, peace-making, optimistic, and forward-thinking.

Negative: pessimistic, judgmental, critical, worrywart, people-pleasing, doubtful, and gossipy.

Hesitate (6)

Meaning: "Hesitate" vibrates to the 6, the number of creativity, the nurturer, and the visionary. Taking on the doubtful and pessimistic energies of the negative 6, "hesitate" is uncertain or unwilling to move forward; "I hesitate to speak my mind in those meetings because I'm not sure how they'll respond to my assertiveness." In the positive, the visionary 6 steps forward to clear the clouds for a better view of what is best in the bigger picture; "I'm not going to hesitate this time; I know it has to be said."

Positive: creative visionary, certainty, balanced, nurturing, peace-making, optimistic, and forward-thinking.

Negative: pessimistic, judgmental, critical, worrywart, people-pleasing, doubtful, and gossipy.

Hinder (4)

Meaning: "Hinder" vibrates to the 4, the solid, stable, practical, and balanced foundation number. "Hinder" means to hold back or delay. The impatience factor associated with the negative 4 vibration gives "hinder" its creative ability to manifest obstacles and fabricate excuses; "Whenever I try to get this done, something always comes up to hinder my progress." In the positive, the enduring and progressive energies of the positive 4 gives "hinder" a means to overcome obstacles; "Nothing is going to hinder me from making it all the way through this course."

Positive: endurance, progress, foundation, practical, balanced, organization, solid, stable, and loyal.

Negative: materialistic, impatient, addictive, instant gratification, and self-absorbed.

Hopeless (9)

Meaning: "Hopeless" vibrates to the 9, the ambitious, ideal-istic, responsible humanitarian number. The 9 is responsi-ble for all the incredible achievements seen in the previous century; everyone born between 1889 and 1999 had at least one 9 in their date of birth. In the negative, the 9 sees things in black and white. With this mindset, things can seem impossible or hopeless; "It's hopeless. I don't think I'll ever get in." In the positive, the 9 is ambitious to change the impossible or the hopeless into idealistic potential; "She's not a hopeless case. I can see the glimmer in her eye and that's enough for me to believe."

Positive: humanitarian, ambitious, responsible, justice-seeking, idealistic, and unselfish.

Negative: driven, opinionated, judgmental, critical, black and white, and narrow-minded.

Horrible (6)

Meaning: "Horrible" vibrates to the 6, the number of creativity, the nurturer, and the visionary. The judgmental and critical energies of the negative 6 make "horrible" a harsh and over-the-top label; "She's just a horrible, horrible person!" In the positive, the balanced, optimistic, and greater vision energy of the 6 allows for more flexibility and possibility; "I have a feeling she's not as horrible as she seems."

Positive: creative visionary, certainty, balanced, nurturing, peace-making, optimistic, and forward-thinking.

Negative: pessimistic, judgmental, critical, worrywart, people-pleasing, doubtful, and gossipy.

Hurt (4)

Meaning: "Hurt" vibrates to the 4, the solid, stable, practical, and balanced foundation number. With the loyal 4 as the base vibration, "hurt" is offended or wounded energy in the negative, playing the role of victim; "I'm hurt that she would leave me out." In the positive, "hurt" shows the enduring, progressive, and balanced side of the 4; "He hurt me deeply, but I'm not going to let it stop me from loving again."

Positive: endurance, progress, foundation, practical, balanced, organization, solid, stable, and loyal.

Negative: materialistic, impatient, addictive, instant gratification, and self-absorbed.

Ignorant (8)

Meaning: "Ignorant" vibrates to the 8, the number of wisdom, independence, confidence, and manifestation. As the most active soul-plane number, 8 has a direct link to the spiritual realm, creating a sense of wholeness and completeness. In the negative, the 8 is bossy, selfish, and attention-seeking, fitting with the word "ignorant"; "Can you believe how ignorant he was to her? He's so self-centered!" Even in the positive, "ignorant" can have an overtone of selfishness as the number of wisdom can make 8 seem like a bit of a know-it-all who is occasionally wrong; "I'm sorry if I came across as ignorant. I jumped to conclusions."

Positive: wise, confident, assertive, independent, manifesting, assured, and loving.

Negative: detached, selfish, greedy, dominating, bossy, and attention-seeking.

Impossible (2)

Meaning: "Impossible" vibrates to the 2, the number of intuition, sensitivity, cooperation, and dualistic energy. In the negative, the dualistic energy of the 2 creates a separation between what you want to do and what you believe you can do; "My boss is impossible to deal with; I give up trying to get through to him." Where 1 is the isolated stand-alone number, the double 1 make the number 2, which is a pair or team. In the positive, the intuitive, harmony-seeking, and cooperative 2 stresses nothing is impossible if you work together; "It's not impossible if you allow me to help you."

Positive: balance, cooperation, sensitive, intuitive, supportive, and harmonious.

Negative: contrast, codependent, uncertain, submissive, passive, and hypersensitive.

Incomplete (4)

Meaning: "Incomplete" vibrates to the 4, the solid, stable, practical, and balanced foundation number. The negative 4 tends to lose momentum easily, being the impatient, self-absorbed, and instant gratification-seeking number. Incomplete goals are common with the negative 4 energy; "My book is still incomplete. I've been picking away at it for years, but can never manage to finish it." In the positive, the enduring, progressive, balanced, and organized 4 doesn't leave much of anything incomplete. "I don't want to see this project remain incomplete and collecting dust. It's a much-needed concept."

Positive: endurance, progress, foundation, practical, balanced, organization, solid, stable, and loyal.

Negative: materialistic, impatient, addictive, instant gratification, and self-absorbed.

Indecisive (9)

Meaning: "Indecisive" vibrates to the 9, the ambitious, ideal-istic, responsible humanitarian number. The 9 is responsi-ble for all the incredible achievements seen in the previous century; everyone born between 1889 and 1999 had at least one 9 in their date of birth. The 9 is the most active mental number, the highest change vibration, and consid-ered the "big dreamer." In the negative, "indecisive" is fo-cused through the idealism of 9, but from a critical and narrow-minded perspective. Instead of the open, big-dreamer energy, uncertainty is formed from the black-and-white vantage point; "I just don't know what the right answer is, I'm so indecisive." In the positive, "indecisive" turns humanitarian and less closed-minded, creating hesi-tancy only because you want to do the right thing for all in-volved; "I'm indecisive about taking the job that requires extra travel because I want what's best for the whole family."

Positive: humanitarian, ambitious, responsible, justice-seeking, idealistic, and unselfish.

Negative: driven, opinionated, judgmental, critical, black and white, and narrow-minded.

Inferior (8)

Meaning: "Inferior" vibrates to the 8, the number of wisdom, independence, confidence, and manifestation. As the most active soul-plane number, 8 has a direct link to the spiritual realm, creating a sense of wholeness and completeness. In the negative, the 8 can feel inferior. Even though it is the number of wisdom, it has lost sight of the innate wisdom it carries; "I secretly think I'm inferior to the other scientists on the team because I came from a family of high-school dropouts." In the positive, the wise 8 knows better and "inferior" is nothing more than a fleeting moment of negativity; "He tried to make me feel inferior but I could see it was his own insecurities shining through his words."

Positive: wise, confident, assertive, independent, manifesting, assured, and loving.

Negative: detached, selfish, greedy, dominating, bossy, and attention-seeking.

Insecure (4)

Meaning: "Insecure" vibrates to the 4, the solid, stable, practical, and balanced foundation number. In the negative, the 4 lacks the stability and balanced energy it uses to be the grounded foundation number. The 4 can be insecure when working through the negative traits of impatience, materialism, and self-absorption; "I'm so insecure around the popular girls. They'll never accept me—ever." In the positive, the enduring, stable, and progressive 4 takes strides to move past the moments of insecurity; "I'm insecure around Ted because he's so competitive, but I can't let that ruin our friendship."

Positive: endurance, progress, foundation, practical, balanced, organization, solid, stable, and loyal.

Negative: materialistic, impatient, addictive, instant gratification, and self-absorbed.

Jealous (2)

Meaning: "Jealous" vibrates to the 2, the number of intuition, sensitivity, cooperation, and dualistic energy. In the negative, the dualistic energy of the 2 creates a perceived separation between you and the cause of your jealousy; "I'm so jealous of my sister's relationship with Dad. We'll never be that close." In the positive, the supportive and cooperative 2 does not seek out the spotlight or demand attention in the same way as the separated 2 in the negative; "I know I shouldn't be jealous of her achievements. My path is different and I have my own achievements to reach."

Positive: balance, cooperation, sensitive, intuitive, supportive, and harmonious.

Negative: contrast, codependent, uncertain, submissive, passive, and hypersensitive.

Judge (2)

Meaning: "Judge" vibrates to the 2, the number of intuition, sensitivity, cooperation, and dualistic energy. In the negative, the dualistic energy of the 2 creates a perceived separation between you and whatever you judge; "I don't want to judge her too quickly, but she makes it pretty clear she doesn't like us." In the positive, the balanced, cooperative, and supportive 2, the number of intuition, sees less of a separation, creating a softened stance on "judge"; "I'm going to hold my judgment until I meet her in person. I'm sure she's different off camera."

Positive: balance, cooperation, sensitive, intuitive, supportive, and harmonious.

Negative: contrast, codependent, uncertain, submissive, passive, and hypersensitive.

Lack (9)

Meaning: "Lack" vibrates to the 9, the ambitious, idealistic, responsible humanitarian number. The 9 is responsible for all the incredible achievements seen in the previous century; everyone born between 1889 and 1999 had at least one 9 in their date of birth. The 9 is the most active mental number, the highest change vibration, and considered the "big dreamer." In the negative, "lack" is cloaked with the judgmental and critical side of the 9; "I lack the support I need to do this right." In the positive, the ambitious and idealistic energies of the 9 step up to the plate, turning "lack" into a tool or motivating factor to move forward; "I may lack the know-how but not the drive to learn."

Positive: humanitarian, ambitious, responsible, justice-seeking, idealistic, and unselfish.

Negative: driven, opinionated, judgmental, critical, black and white, and narrow-minded.

Limit (9)

Meaning: "Limit" vibrates to the 9, the ambitious, idealistic, responsible humanitarian number. The 9 is responsible for all the incredible achievements seen in the previous century; everyone born between 1889 and 1999 had at least one 9 in their date of birth. The 9 is the most active mental number, the highest change vibration, and considered the "big dreamer." As the opinionated and critical negative 9, placing a limit on anything is common; "I've got to limit my time with her; she's a bad influence." In the positive, the idealistic, ambitious humanitarian sees a limit as a challenge to overcome; "There is no limit on the things you can achieve if you set your mind to it."

Positive: humanitarian, ambitious, responsible, justice-seeking, idealistic, and unselfish.

Negative: driven, opinionated, judgmental, critical, black and white, and narrow-minded.

Lost (3)

Meaning: "Lost" vibrates to the 3, the intellectual number of imagination, memory, and inspiration. The 3 also represents unity or coming together. In the negative, the self-doubting and self-critical 3 makes it easy to feel lost in ways big or small; "I'm lost. This new math concept is way over my head." In the positive, the intelligent and inspirational will infuse optimism into "lost"; "All is not lost. You'll get it, I promise."

Positive: analytical, intelligent, humorous, social, sensitive, observant, unity, and inspirational.

Negative: critical, vain, grandeur, self-doubting, self-critical, overanalyzing, and indecisive.

Maybe (1)

Meaning: "Maybe" vibrates to the number 1, with the isolated pioneer, new beginnings, and trailblazing energy. The 1 is the only number not divisible by any other number so it is a stand-alone energy. "Maybe" in the negative utilizes the isolated and egocentric qualities of the 1. In the negative, the focus of the 1 is exterior or ego-focused, inhibiting the access of deeper truth within to make a definitive decision; "Maybe I will, I just don't know what to do." In the positive, the 1 affords potential or possibility for "maybe" as the redirection of energy is put on the determined, pioneering side of the 1; "There's no 'maybe' about it, I will pass this test."

Positive: verbal self-expression, initiate, action, ambitious, determined, and pioneering.

Negative: aggressive, egocentric, overly driven, self-absorbed, overachieving, and single-focused.

Need (1)

Meaning: "Need" vibrates to the number 1, with the isolated pioneer, new beginnings, and trailblazing energy. The 1 is the only number not divisible by any other number so it is a stand-alone energy. In the negative, the single-focused, aggressive, and egocentric 1 works to consume and collect, needing more to achieve, forgetting the true nature of the 1, which is a stand-alone number, and perfect as it is. In the positive, the isolated pioneering 1 is in need of nothing to feel whole and complete; "There are a lot of things I want but nothing I need."

Positive: verbal self-expression, initiate, action, ambitious, determined, and pioneering.

Negative: aggressive, egocentric, overly driven, self-absorbed, overachieving, and single-focused.

Never (1)

Meaning: "Never" vibrates to the number 1, with the isolated pioneer, new beginnings, and trailblazing energy. The 1 is the only number not divisible by any other number so it is a stand-alone energy. "Never" emphasizes the isolated and egocentric qualities of the 1. In the negative, the focus of the 1 is exterior or ego-focused, limiting possibility or potential; "She'll never take the leap; she doesn't have it in her." In the positive, the pioneering and trailblazing 1 takes charge; "Never say never!"

Positive: verbal self-expression, initiate, action, ambitious, determined, and pioneering.

Negative: aggressive, egocentric, overly driven, self-absorbed, overachieving, and single-focused.

No (2)

Meaning: "No" vibrates to the 2, the number of intuition, sensitivity, cooperation, and dualistic energy. In the negative, the dualistic energy of the 2 creates a separation or a desire to be separate from whatever you are saying no to. This separate energy also gives "no" a definitive and firm response; "No, I'm not coming with you." In the positive, "no" has a similar stance with expressing the desire to be separate, but with overtones of thoughtfulness, sensitivity, intuition, and harmony; "Thank you for inviting me, but I have to say no to your offer."

Positive: balance, cooperation, sensitive, intuitive, supportive, and harmonious.

Negative: contrast, codependent, uncertain, submissive, passive, and hypersensitive.

No Way (6)

Meaning: "No way" vibrates to the 6, the number of creativity, the nurturer, and the visionary. The judgmental and critical energies of the negative 6 make the phrase "no way" a powerfully pessimistic statement limiting all possibility; "There is no way I'm going to get this done." In the positive, the optimistic, forward-thinking visionary opens the doorway to possibility; "There may seem like no way to make this happen now, but where there's a will, there's a way!"

Positive: creative visionary, certainty, balanced, nurturing, peace-making, optimistic, and forward-thinking.

Negative: pessimistic, judgmental, critical, worrywart, people-pleasing, doubtful, and gossipy.

Not (4)

Meaning: "Not" vibrates to the 4, the solid, stable, practical, and balanced foundation number. In the negative, depending on the use of "not," the focus can be on the impatience or loyalty of the 4; "I'm not going reach my goal at this rate" or "She is not going to get away with lying to me." In the positive, the solid, stable, practical 4 says "not" is just a hurdle to overcome on the path; "C'mon, it's not that bad, let's keep moving forward" or "I'm not going to let a little setback stop me."

Positive: endurance, progress, foundation, practical, balanced, organization, solid, stable, and loyal.

Negative: materialistic, impatient, addictive, instant gratification, and self-absorbed.

Pain (4)

Meaning: "Pain" vibrates to the 4, the solid, stable, practical, and balanced foundation number. Pain, whether it is mental, emotional, or physical, is a result of some form of loss or trauma. In the negative, the 4 loses the balanced and solid energy it possesses and takes on the addictive, instant gratification, and self-absorbed traits to deal with or process pain; "I just can't deal with the pain of this loss right now. All I want to do is sleep." In the positive, 4 is enduring, progressive, practical, and stable in its outlook on pain; "No pain, no gain!"

Positive: endurance, progress, foundation, practical, balanced, organization, solid, stable, and loyal.

Negative: materialistic, impatient, addictive, instant gratification, and self-absorbed.

Problem (9)

Meaning: "Problem" vibrates to the 9, the ambitious, idealistic, responsible humanitarian number. The 9 is responsible for all the incredible achievements seen in the previous century; everyone born between 1889 and 1999 had at least one 9 in their date of birth. The 9 is the most active mental number, the highest change vibration, and considered the "big dreamer." In the negative, the right-and-wrong, justice-seeking energy of the 9 makes "problem" a matter-of-fact or black-and-white issue; "The problem is that she's too shy." In the positive, "problem" embraces the ambitious and idealistic energies of the 9, turning "problem" into more of a challenge to be overcome; "That's no problem, I can handle it."

Positive: humanitarian, ambitious, responsible, justice-seeking, idealistic, and unselfish.

Negative: driven, opinionated, judgmental, critical, black and white, and narrow-minded.

Regret (1)

Meaning: "Regret" vibrates to the number 1, with the isolated pioneer, new beginnings, and trailblazing energy. The 1 is the only number not divisible by any other number so it is a stand-alone energy. In the negative, "regret" emphasizes the isolated and egocentric qualities of the 1 and does not allow for seeing the deeper meaning or truth in the cause of regret; "I regret saying those hurtful things in anger but I don't know how to make it right with her." In the positive, the 1 adds the determined and initiating energies to help resolve lingering regret; "I regret blurting out that embarrassing statement because it's not what I really meant, but I'm determined to set things straight."

Positive: verbal self-expression, initiate, action, ambitious, determined, and pioneering.

Negative: aggressive, egocentric, overly driven, self-absorbed, overachieving, and single-focused.

Risk (3)

Meaning: "Risk" vibrates to the 3, the intellectual number of imagination, memory, and inspiration. The 3 also represents unity or coming together. In the negative, the self-doubting and self-critical 3 isn't willing to take the risk; "I just can't risk being hurt again right now." In the positive, the optimistic, imaginative, and inspirational 3 is willing to risk it all; "Let's do this! I just know this idea is going to go viral."

Positive: analytical, intelligent, humorous, social, sensitive, observant, unity, and inspirational.

Negative: critical, vain, grandeur, self-doubting, self-critical, overanalyzing, and indecisive.

Shouldn't (5)

Meaning: "Shouldn't" vibrates to the 5, the number of the heart, emotions, and compassionate "freedom of expression" energy. In the negative, the dominating and bossy energies take over and "shouldn't" is less centered in the more positive-focused, loving, and passionate 5 energy; "You shouldn't wear that; it doesn't look appropriate for your body type." In the positive, the loving, compassionate, flexible 5 energy may make a heart-centered suggestion but doesn't push it on anyone, allowing for freedom of expression; "I'm not saying you should or you shouldn't, I'm just sharing what I would do. It's your choice in the end."

Positive: loving, sensitive, irregular, artistic, freedom-seeking, passionate, and flexible.

Negative: uncertain, power-hungry, dominating, bossy, withdrawn, and moody.

Struggle (1)

Meaning: "Struggle" vibrates to the number 1, with the isolated pioneer, new beginnings, and trailblazing energy. The 1 is the only number not divisible by any other number so it is a stand-alone energy. "Struggle" emphasizes the isolated and separated qualities of the 1 in the negative. When we feel separated or isolated, we believe there is more of a struggle ahead of us; "I had to struggle for everything I've accomplished with no help from anyone." In the positive, "struggle" is fuel for motivation of the trailblazing and driven 1; "I'm determined to stop the struggle and start living."

Positive: verbal self-expression, initiate, action, ambitious, determined, and pioneering.

Negative: aggressive, egocentric, overly driven, self-absorbed, overachieving, and single-focused.

Stuck (2)

Meaning: "Stuck" vibrates to the 2, the number of intuition, sensitivity, cooperation, and dualistic energy. In the negative, the dualistic energy of the 2 creates a separation and a feeling of being stuck; "With all these bills, I'll be stuck in this job forever." In the positive, the 2 strives to be a supportive, balanced, and cooperative energy or a team player; "stuck" then becomes more of a wedge to be removed rather than a definite line separating sides; "I'm stuck on this problem, but I know just the resource that can shed some light on it."

Positive: balance, cooperation, sensitive, intuitive, supportive, and harmonious.

Negative: contrast, codependent, uncertain, submissive, passive, and hypersensitive.

Suppressed (7)

Meaning: "Suppressed" vibrates to the 7, the deep, philosophical, teaching and learning, truth-seeker energy. As the most active physical-plane number, the 7 desires to be free to seek the deeper meaning in all things. In the negative, the stubbornness of the 7 shines bright, resisting stagnancy or being suppressed in any way; "I feel like my true talents and gifts are being suppressed in this job." In the positive, being suppressed is viewed as a possible piece of the puzzle or deeper truth; "I'm a bit suppressed in my creativity at the moment with other things going on in my life, but I know I'll get my writing groove back as soon as things are less intense."

Positive: wise, contemplative, achiever, truth-seeking, determined, and hands-on.

Negative: stubborn, overactive, distrustful, hesitant, skeptical, and loner.

Unbelievable (4)

Meaning: "Unbelievable" vibrates to the 4, the solid, stable, practical, and balanced foundation number. In the negative, the focus is on the very practical, grounded, and often skeptical energy of the 4, closing the door on whatever is considered to be unbelievable; "I'm not buying his performance. It's too unbelievable to be the real deal." In the positive, the steadfast and hardworking side of the 4 leaves the door open to work toward achieving what seems out of reach; "It's too unbelievable to be true, but stranger things have happened."

Positive: balance, cooperation, sensitive, intuitive, supportive, and harmonious.

Negative: uncertain, power-hungry, dominating, bossy, withdrawn, and moody.

Won't (9)

Meaning: "Won't" vibrates to the 9, the ambitious, idealistic, responsible humanitarian number. The 9 is responsible for all the incredible achievements seen in the previous century; everyone born between 1889 and 1999 had at least one 9 in their date of birth. The 9 is the most active mental number, the highest change vibration, and considered the "big dreamer." In the negative, "won't" gathers its strength from the black-and-white or right-and-wrong justice-seeking 9; "I won't do it, no way!" In the positive, "won't" is optimistic or idealistic in outlook; "I won't let a little setback stop me."

Positive: humanitarian, ambitious, responsible, justice-seeking, idealistic, and unselfish.

Negative: driven, opinionated, judgmental, critical, black and white, and narrow-minded.

Glossary

destiny: a decided or predetermined path; fate.

energy: the capacity of a physical system to do work; power.

essence: the basis, core, or true fundamental nature of something.

frequency: the number of times a vibration repeats itself in a specified time dictates its frequency, often measured in hertz; for example, we tune in our radio to the particular radio frequency the station is broadcasting.

manifest: to make clear, noticeable, and distinguishable to the senses; to bring to awareness.

metaphysical: the transcendent, or referring to something beyond what the traditional five senses can perceive.

numerology: a system utilizing numbers to represent energy patterns in all things; the science of numbers as originally developed by Greek mathematician and philosopher Pythagoras, who believed all things are numbers at their base.

reality: the quality or state of being real or true.

vibration: a rapid linear motion of a particle or an elastic solid about an equilibrium position.

Recommended Reading

Emoto, Masaru. *Hidden Messages in Water*. Hillsboro, OR: Beyond Words Publishing, 2004.

Losier, Michael J. *Law of Attraction: The Science of Attracting More of What You Want and Less of What You Don't*. New York: Grand Central Life & Style, 2010.

Millman, Dan. *The Life You Were Born to Live: A Guide to Finding Your Life Purpose*. Tiburon, CA: HJ Kramer, 1995.

Phillips, David A. *The Complete Book of Numerology: Discovering the Inner Self*. Carlsbad, CA: Hay House, 2005.

Virtue, Doreen. *Angel Numbers 101: The Meaning of 111, 123, 444, and Other Number Sequences*. Carlsbad, CA: Hay House, 2008.

Virtue, Doreen, and Grant Virtue. *Angel Words: Visual Evidence of How Words Can Be Angels In Your Life*. Carlsbad, CA: Hay House, 2010.

Endnotes

1. David Bohm, *Wholeness and the Implicate Order* (New York: Routledge, 2002).

2. "Work, Energy, and Power: Basic Terminology and Concepts," The Physics Classroom, http://www.physicsclass-room.com/Class/energy/u5l1d.cfm.

3. Andrew Zimmerman Jones with Daniel Robbins, "String Theory for Dummies," For Dummies, http://www.dum-mies.com/how-to/content/string-theory-for-dummies-cheat-sheet.html.

4. "History of Language," History World, http://www.his-toryworld.net/wrldhis/PlainTextHistories.asp?history-id=ab13#ixzz28XQHvkus.

5. Gautam Naik, "The Mother of All Languages," *Wall Street Journal*, April 15, 2011, http://online.wsj.com/article/SB 10001424052748704547604576262572791243528.html.

6. David Caplan, "Language and the Brain," *Harvard Mahoney Neuroscience Institute Letter* (Fall 1995) 4:4, http://www.hms.harvard.edu/hmni/On_The_Brain/Volume04/Number4/F95Lang.html.

7. Schrauf, Robert W. and Julia Sanchez (2004), "The preponderance of negative emotion words across generations and across cultures," *Journal of Multilingual and Multicultural Development*, 25:(2–3), 266–284.

8. Lee Dye, "Study: Negative Words Dominate Language," ABC News, February 2, 2005, http://abcnews.go.com/Technology/DyeHard/story?id=460987&page=1.

9. "Innate Behavior," http://users.rcn.com/jkimball.ma.ultranet/BiologyPages/I/InnateBehavior.html.

10. Christine Comaford, "Got Inner Peace? 5 Ways to Get It NOW," *Forbes*, April 4, 2012, http://www.forbes.com/sites/christinecomaford/2012/04/04/got-inner-peace-5-ways-to-get-it-now/.

11. *Stanford Encyclopedia of Philosophy*, s.v. "Pythagoras," http://plato.stanford.edu/entries/pythagoras/.

12. Mark Pearlman, "Gematria: 2009 by the Numbers," *Jewish Journal*, January 5, 2010, http://www.jewishjournal.com/opinion/article/ultimate_decade_review_the_gematria_revealed_20100105.

13. Gematria chart, http://www.inner.org/gematria/gemchart.htm.

14. Michelle Arbeau, "Power of Numbers: Gain Clarity, Insight & Transform Your Life NOW!" http://michellearbeau.com/wp-content/uploads/2010/11/Power-of-Numbers-Manual1.pdf.

15. Ronald Segal, *The Black Diaspora: Five Centuries of the Black Experience Outside Africa*. New York: Farrar, Straus and Giroux, 1995, p. 4. "It is now estimated that 11,863,000 slaves were shipped across the Atlantic [Note in original: Paul E. Lovejoy, "The Impact of the Atlantic Slave Trade on Africa: A Review of the Literature," *Journal of African History* 30 (1989), p. 368.] ... It is widely conceded that further revisions are more likely to be upward than downward."

16. "Reduce, Reuse, Recycle." http://www.planetpals.com/recyclesymbols.html.

To Write to the Author

If you wish to contact the author or would like more information about this book, please write to the author in care of Llewellyn Worldwide Ltd. and we will forward your request. Both the author and publisher appreciate hearing from you and learning of your enjoyment of this book and how it has helped you. Llewellyn Worldwide Ltd. cannot guarantee that every letter written to the author can be answered, but all will be forwarded. Please write to:

Michelle Arbeau
⁒ Llewellyn Worldwide
2143 Wooddale Drive
Woodbury, MN 55125-2989

Please enclose a self-addressed stamped envelope for reply, or $1.00 to cover costs. If outside the U.S.A., enclose an international postal reply coupon.